The New Americans
Recent Immigration and American Society

Edited by
Steven J. Gold and Rubén G. Rumbaut

A Series from LFB Scholarly

Educational Attainment in Immigrant Families
Community Context and Family background

Gabriella C. Gonzalez

LFB Scholarly Publishing LLC
New York 2005

Library of Congress Cataloging-in-Publication Data

Gonzalez, Gabriella C., 1972-
    Educational attainment in immigrant families : community context
and family background / Gabriella C. Gonzalez.
        p. cm. -- (The new Americans)
    Includes bibliographical references and index.
    ISBN 1-59332-101-5 (alk. paper)
    1. Children of immigrants--Education--United States. 2. Educational
attainment--United States. I. Title. II. Series: New Americans (LFB
Scholarly Publishing LLC)
    LC3746.G66 2005
    371.826'912'0973--dc22

                                    2005021181

ISBN 1-59332-101-5

Printed on acid-free 250-year-life paper.

Manufactured in the United States of America.

For Joaquin Montelibano,

child of a "combined" family

Table of Contents

List of Tables

List of Figures

xi

Acknowledgments

I am grateful for the timely funding by a grant from the American Educational Research Association which receives funds for its "AERA Grants Program" from the National Center for Education Statistics and the Office of Educational Research and Improvement (U.S. Department of Education) and the National Science Foundation under NSF Grant #RED–9452861 to complete the research in this book while I was at the Department of Sociology at Harvard University. Opinions reflect those of the author and do not necessarily reflect those of the granting agencies.

I would like to thank members of the sociology department at Harvard University who were instrumental in the development of the ideas in this piece: Sandy Jencks, Orlando Patterson, Aage B. Sorensen, Mary C. Waters, and Christopher Winship. Cheri Minton, data manager at the sociology department at Harvard University, provided early help with data from the U.S. Census and Irene Bloemraad, Bayliss Camp, Susan Dumais, Devon Johnson, Ziad Munson, and Monica McDermott read early drafts.

I would also like to acknowledge the support of Charles Goldman, Dominic Brewer, and Sue Bodilly in the Education Unit at RAND who gave me valuable time and support to complete this book. Sheila Kirby and Sandraluz Lara-Cinisomo provided valuable feedback and suggestions for improvement. M. Yvonne Gonzalez and Jesse Reyes edited early drafts and Louis Ramirez deftly handled a difficult final review. Their reading of drafts of this manuscript improved it greatly, for which I am deeply grateful. However, I claim full responsibility for any errors or faults within.

Preface

Social stratification research consistently links a person's social and economic position to his or her parents' education and occupation (e.g., Blau & Duncan, 1967). However, this traditional status attainment literature does not give adequate attention to immigrants to the United States who have arrived since the 1965 Family Reunification Act. Using data from the 1990 U.S. Census, International Data on Educational Attainment (2000), and the National Education Longitudinal Study (1988-1994), this book fills the gaps in previous status attainment research of immigrants by examining how differential experiences of immigrant parents in the labor markets of their country of origin and in the United States affect their children's schooling experiences.

The central question I ask is which factor is more important for students: the family's status before arriving in the United States or after arriving? I argue that knowing a parent's education and occupational status before arriving in the United States, in addition to understanding the possible mediating effects of the ethnic enclave is central to understanding how a student will approach schooling. This book analyzes the differences in likelihood to enter post-secondary schooling among white, black, Latino and Asian children who have two parents who are immigrants, only one parent who is foreign-born or both parents who are native-born.

I find that children in homes with two parents who are immigrants go farther in school than their counterparts in homes with one or no parents who are immigrants. Concurrent with prevailing research, children in homes with one parent who is an immigrant have educational trajectories similar to their counterparts in homes with no immigrant parents, rather than their counterparts in homes with two immigrant parents. The parents' educational attainment and the social capital of the family are clear predictors in determining how far children of native parents go in school, but are not as strong determinants for children of immigrant parents. I also find ethnic differences in the educational attainment of a child of two immigrant parents: Puerto Rican, Mexican, and Filipino children do not go as far in school as white children and Chinese-descent children go farther than white children, even when we consider the immigrant parents' pre-arrival education and the post-arrival community context. To explain these differences, I examine if parental involvement affects how far in school children go. I determine that parental supervision at home has an effect on the educational attainment of children in immigrant, combined, and native families.

This book will enable educators and policy makers to understand the interactions among pre-arrival social status of an immigrant family, the community context in which a family finds itself, and the involvement of parents at home to affect a child's educational trajectory. It is necessary for educators and policy makers to differentiate between students with two immigrant parents and one immigrant parent when considering how best to educate children of immigrants. Although from the same ethnic background, the effects of parents' educational attainment and community context differ greatly suggesting that their needs in the classroom will differ and must be addressed.

CHAPTER 1

Understanding Status Attainment Processes within Native and Immigrant Families

For many decades the primary debate surrounding immigration policy in the United States has been about the consequences of immigration on the national economy: how well immigrant adults perform in the labor market, to what extent immigrant adults affect the employment potential for native adults, or whether immigrant adults contribute or detract from the economy. While these concerns are important topics that continue to be controversial, a recent issue facing education policymakers has been the growing school-age population of children who are either immigrants themselves or children of immigrants (Suárez-Orozco & Suárez-Orozco, 2001; Zhou, 1997). Understanding the potential of these children to succeed in school is important in answering questions about whether immigration as a whole contributes to our economy, or if immigrants as a sub-group population are succeeding in the labor market.

An abundance of studies exists that examine differences in educational attainment among immigrant generations to determine which generation "succeeds" more than another and why. The focus on educational attainment is primarily due to the fact that educational attainment can be linked to future earnings success, and much of the income inequality among groups in the labor market is due to educational attainment inequality. Yet the large body of research pertaining to immigrants and education has not provided conclusive evidence about the intergenerational transmission of status. This is largely due to three methodological weaknesses. First, it uses cross-sectional quantitative and qualitative studies to estimate what are essentially longitudinal patterns. Second, it does not fully define socioeconomic status. And third, it lacks a consistent analysis of the role of ethnic enclaves.

The research presented in this book improves previous research in two ways. First, the longitudinal nature of the data I employ helps to analyze how well immigrants are performing in school and in the labor market compared to their native-born counterparts, which previous cross-sectional analyses have failed to do. Second, I reconsider current status attainment models for immigrants by constructing a family background variable that includes parents' pre-arrival education. Knowing a parent's educational attainment and occupation before arriving in the United States, in addition to understanding the possible mediating effects of the ethnic enclave, is central to understanding how a student in an immigrant household will approach schooling. The analyses within this book examine these interactions to develop a more accurate educational attainment model that includes the pre-arrival education of the immigrant parents while also investigating the role of the post-arrival occupational status and community context of the family. With this new model, I am able to develop a stronger understanding of status attainment patterns for immigrants and their children in the United States.

We are now at a point when we can look at the educational attainment, and thus potential labor market success, of children of post-1965 immigrant households. The children who immigrated in the 1970s and 1980s or who have parents who immigrated since the 1965 Family Reunification Act are just entering the labor market pool now. Thus, the timing of this study offers valuable findings for immigrant intergenerational status attainment—a particularly important topic given the growing numbers of immigrant students in our nation's schools. These status attainment patterns will determine whether a family or particular immigrant group will economically or socially assimilate to the prevailing labor market and social structures in American society; that is, whether the family or group will "succeed."

FOCUS OF BOOK

This study investigates the predictors of educational attainment of the growing Asian and Latino school-aged population, many of whom are either immigrants themselves or the children of immigrants. Using data from the 2000 International Data on Educational Attainment, the 2002 March Current Population Survey, various years of the United States Decennial Census, and the first four waves of the National Education Longitudinal Study (1988-1994), this study examines how the experiences of immigrant parents in the labor markets of both their country of origin and in the United States affect their children's schooling experiences. I compare differences in educational attainment of Asian and Latino children in households in which both parents are immigrants, one parent is an immigrant, or both parents are native-born.

I focus on two questions: Does the educational attainment of immigrant parents explain their child's educational attainment in the same way that the educational attainment of native-born parents often explains differences in the educational attainment of their children? Which factor is more important for the educational attainment of students in households with one or two foreign-born parents: the family's status before arriving in the United States or the context in which the family lives after arriving?

Even though researchers are giving greater attention to the educational needs of students in immigrant households, there has not been a serious commitment to disentangling the effects of structural constraints (community context), individual factors (language ability, minority status, and immigrant status), and family background (parents' education and occupation prior to arriving in the United States) on educational attainment. Much of the present research focuses either on one aspect of these three interrelated characteristics, or on the combination of just two (for example, Buriel & Cardoza, 1988; Portes & MacLeod, 1996; Warren, 1996; Mau, 1997; Bhattacharya, 2000). I devote this book to disentangling these effects. Figure 1.1 illustrates how pre-arrival social status, post-arrival social status, and community context may influence the educational trajectories of children in immigrant households.

Figure 1.1: Effects of Pre-arrival and Post-arrival Social Status of Immigrant Adults on Their Child's Educational Attainment

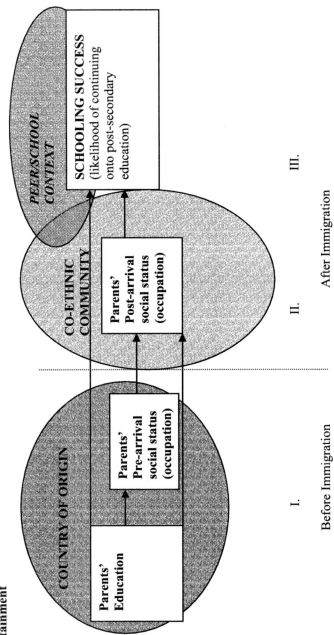

In the remainder of this chapter, I use data from various years of the United States Decennial Census and from the 2002 March Current Population Survey to detail the trends in immigration to the United States over the past century. It is evident from these data that recently arrived immigrants are a heterogeneous group. Most are from Latin America, the Caribbean, or Asia and are disproportionately represented in both the highest and lowest levels of education. They are also highly concentrated in a few states and have higher poverty rates than the native-born population. I then provide a review of prevailing theories of assimilation of immigrant generations into the social and economic structure of the United States, and how the "assimilation" of the family affects the schooling success of children born into immigrant households. I reflect upon the gaps in the current literature of status attainment with an eye toward how the study of children born of immigrant parents can deepen our understanding of educational attainment patterns and the transference of skills from one generation to the next for all children in the United States. The last section provides a guide to the remaining chapters of the book.

RECENT IMMIGRATION TO THE UNITED STATES

The United States is currently experiencing a wave of immigration unprecedented since the early 1900s, with close to six million immigrants having entered in the 1990s and approximately three million from year 2000 to 2002 (Camarota, 1999; 2002). Table 1.1 summarizes the number of immigrants entering during each decade and their percentage of the U.S. population from 1900 to 2000. In 2000, 28.4 million immigrants lived in the United States—a 43 percent increase over 1990 figures (Lollock, 2001; Schmidley, 2001). By 2002, that number increased to 32.5 million immigrants, the largest number ever in the nation's history—an increase of 12.7 million (64.2 percent) above the estimated 19.8 million in the 1990 U.S. Census (Schmidley & Robinson, 2003). In 2002, immigrants accounted for 11.5 percent of the U.S. population—the highest percentage in seven decades.

In 1900, 84.9 percent of immigrants to the United States were from Europe; 1.3 percent from Latin America; 1.2 percent from Asia; and 12.6 percent from all other countries (Lapham, 1993). In the 1950s Europeans, Canadians, New Zealanders, and Australians represented 53 percent of the legal immigrants Latin Americans and Caribbeans accounted for 25 percent, and Asians for six percent. The numbers are quite different today. According to the March 2003 Current Population Survey, 43.2 percent of foreign-born people are from Latin America or South America; 25 percent from Asia; 13.7 percent from Europe; and 10.1 percent from the Caribbean (Larsen, 2004).

Table 1.1: Immigration to the United States over the Last Century

Year	Foreign-born Population*	Percent of U.S. Population
1900	10.4	13.6
1910	13.6	14.7
1920	14.0	13.2
1930	14.3	11.6
1940	11.7	8.8
1950	10.4	6.9
1960	9.7	5.4
1970	9.6	4.8
1980	14.1	6.2
1990	19.8	7.9
2000	28.4	11.1
2002	32.5	11.5

Sources: U.S Census Bureau Decennial Census 1900-2000; 2002 Current Population Survey (from Lollock, 2001, Schmidley, 2001; Lapham, 1993; Camarota, 2002; Schmidley & Robinson, 2002)
*In millions

One reason for the dramatic change in immigrants' region of origin is the Family Reunification Act of 1965, which changed the primary criterion for admission from nationality to family reunification, with a smaller emphasis on needed skills (Usdansky & Espenshade, 2000). Refugees also added substantially to increased immigration, particularly from Cuba and Southeast Asia: about 870,000 of the 2,100,000 refugees who entered the U.S. between 1961 and 1993 were from these geographical areas (Edmonston, 1996).

Table 1.2 shows the top fifteen countries of origin for immigrants in each decade since the 1970s. The 1970s column notes the number of immigrants from a particular country who arrived from 1970 through 1979; the 1980s column presents the number of immigrants who arrived from 1980 through 1989, and so on. The 2000s column shows the number of immigrants who arrived between 2000 and 2002.

Table 1.2: Top Fifteen Sending Countries to the United States[a]

		Year of Entry[b]					
	Pre-1970	1970s	1980s	1990s	2000s	2002 Total	% Imm. Population
Mexico	652	1,350	2,389	4,254	1,014	9,659	29.70
China[c]	137	187	368	607	149	1,449	4.45
Philippines	136	293	488	431	81	1,429	4.39
India	30	145	276	608	246	1,304	4.01
Cuba	344	136	165	213	62	919	2.82
El Salvador	17	102	332	358	60	868	2.67
Vietnam	13	164	264	319	59	819	2.52
S. Korea	59	157	241	215	85	756	2.32
Canada	305	79	96	178	55	714	2.19
D. Republic	67	119	195	241	31	652	2.00
Germany	370	60	52	120	34	638	1.96
Haiti	29	73	191	231	47	569	1.75
Colombia	49	74	122	217	77	540	1.66
Russia	38	49	68	305	47	508	1.56
Guatemala	11	38	125	185	48	407	1.25

Source: U.S. Census Bureau: 2002 Current Population Survey, Annual Social and Economic Data Supplement (from Camarota, 2002 and Schmidley & Robinson, 2003)

[a] Numbers are in thousands

[b] Based on "year of entry" question

[c] Includes Taiwan and Hong Kong

In 2002, Mexicans comprised the largest number of immigrants from any part of the world: 9.4 million people, or almost 30 percent of the immigrants in the United States. Mexico has consistently been a strong supply country for many decades. Other countries, however, have only recently sent relatively large numbers of people to the United States. These include India and China, which surpassed all other countries except Mexico in the 1990s. Before the 1970s, however, the top sending countries to the United States in addition to Mexico were Germany, Cuba, and Canada.

Because immigration from Europe has dwindled to low levels in recent years, the white (non-Hispanic) population is increasingly becoming a native-born population with native-born parents. The Asian population consists predominantly of recent immigrants—more than two-thirds of its members are first or second generation U.S. immigrants—and will continue to be immigrant-centered for the next several decades.[1] Further, more than half of the Hispanic population is in the first and second generation of U.S immigrants. This situation may continue into the future assuming current levels of immigration, fertility, and mortality (Edmonston, 1996).

GEOGRAPHIC CONCENTRATION OF RECENT IMMIGRANTS

Immigrants tend to gravitate to particular regions of the United States. The large increase in immigration, demonstrated in Table 1.1, and the changing composition of immigrants, portrayed in Table 1.2, have placed a concomitant demand on school systems in specific geographic areas because of the density of immigrants. Asian-Americans and Latinos represent the most rapidly growing part of the school-age population. Differing fertility rates, immigration patterns, and age distributions among ethnic minorities suggest that by the year 2030, the U.S. elementary school population could be divided equally between white children and children of all other racial and ethnic groups combined. This "minority" subgroup is expected to outnumber the white subgroup by the year 2050 (Hodgkinson, 1992).

Immigrants, and thus their school-going children, are concentrated in California, New York, Florida, Texas, and Illinois. The foreign-born population constitutes about one-fifth of the school populations in Los Angeles, Miami and San Francisco (McDonnell & Hill, 1993). In 1998, the nearly nine million immigrants in California accounted for 30.3 percent of the nation's total immigrant population. New York has the next highest percent of immigrants (13.8), followed by Florida (8.8 percent), Texas (8.8 percent), Illinois (4.5 percent), and New Jersey

(4.5 percent). These six states account for 71 percent of the immigrant population, but only 39 percent of the nation's total population (Camarota, 1999). Table 1.3 charts the concentration of immigrants by state, listing the top receiving states in the United States as of 2000. It is evident that these states have large concentrations of immigrants. For example, almost one-quarter of California's population is immigrant—of whom one-quarter arrived in the 1990s. Twenty percent of New York's population is immigrant—about one-third of whom arrived in the 1990s. In these select states, the concentration and steep rise of immigrant populations in the past decade makes it difficult for resources to stay abreast of population growth and the community's needs. In fact, the burden is heaviest on the school systems in these states that have to support large and rapid increases in school-age children due to immigration.

Table 1.3: States with the Highest Percentage of Foreign-Born

STATE	% of State Population	Total Imm. Population[a]	1990s Arrivals[a]
California	25.9	8,781	2,158
New York	19.6	3,634	1,231
Florida	18.4	2,768	747
Hawaii	16.1	205	93
New Jersey	14.9	1,208	383
Arizona	12.9	638	247
Texas	12.2	2,443	740
Illinois	9.5	1,155	240

Source: U.S. Census Bureau Decennial Census 2000
[a] Numbers are in thousands

In addition to being highly concentrated in certain states, immigrants often reside together in the same or adjacent communities. Ethnic plurality is a distinctive, yet common, feature of today's immigrant neighborhood (Zhou, 2001), indicating that a single national-origin group no longer dominates the new immigrant enclaves as in the turn of the century. Immigrant families are living in more ethnically mixed neighborhoods as compared to native families, but with their fellow immigrant counterparts. In Figure 1.2, I use the geographic boundary of zip code to delineate a community. Overall, we see that immigrants and native-born reside in very different settings. For example, immigrants live in zip code areas with greater ethnic heterogeneity than their native-born counterparts do. The mean percentage of zip code inhabitants who are of the same ethnicity as the respondent (co-ethnics) is 36 percent for immigrants, compared to 79 percent for natives. Conversely, immigrants tend to live among their foreign peers: 33 percent compared to less than five percent for natives.

Figure 1.2: Geographic Concentration of Immigrants

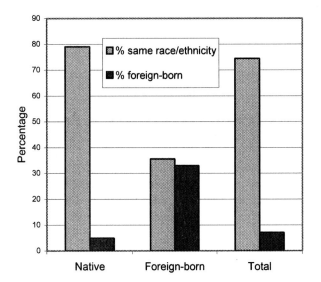

Note: Sample is adults aged 25 or over who are not enrolled in school
Source: U.S. Census Bureau Decennial Census 2000

During the 1990s, U.S. public schools have seen an increase of almost one million immigrant students, approximately 5.5 percent of the public school population. The significant effect immigration has had on the size of the school-age population in top receiving states is clearly demonstrated in Table 1.4. Although nationally 11.5 percent of the total population in the United States is foreign-born, about 18 percent of children ages 5-17 have an immigrant mother and approximately 19 percent of children ages 0-4 have immigrant mothers. Similarly, while 26 percent of California's population is foreign-born, almost one-half of school-age children in California have an immigrant mother; almost one-third of school-age children in Arizona have a mother born outside of the United States, compared to 13 percent of the state population being foreign-born.

Table 1.4: Percentage of School-Age Children with Foreign-Born Mothers

State	Age 0-4	Age 5-17
All States	19.2%	18.3%
California	43.5	44.6
Arizona	30.0	29.2
New Jersey	27.1	23.6
Florida	25.7	25.6
New York	25.1	28.1
Texas	26.1	25.4
Massachusetts	16.2	15.6
Maryland	19.9	22.5

Source: U.S. Census Bureau: 2002 Current Population Study, Annual Social and Economic Data Supplement

CHALLENGES FACING STUDENTS OF IMMIGRANT PARENTS

One of the challenges currently facing many educators is providing equal educational opportunities to students of immigrant parents (McDonnell & Hill, 1993; Vernez, 1996). Students in immigrant households face unique barriers in the classroom (Rong & Hickey, 1998; Rong & Preissler, 1998; Perkins, 2000), which include:

- *Previous Educational Background.* Foreign-born students may have limited schooling in their home countries or interruptions in their schooling because of immigration (McCargo, 1999; Crandall et al., 1985). They may not be accustomed to learning from a book or to using the "tools of the trade" such as a ruler, calculator, or protractor (Genesee, 1999). In addition, they may have limited literacy skills in their native language if they did not have any formal schooling in their country of origin (Morse, 1990).
- *Age of Entry into School.* Immigrant students enter U.S. schools at every grade level and at various times during the academic year. A teacher may need to accommodate a mixed age group with different maturity and developmental levels (Genesee, 1999).
- *Cultural Conflicts.* Students may have difficulty balancing the value systems of their native culture, present at home, with those of the dominant culture, prevailing at school (Ghasarian, 1995; Lucas, 1996). The conflict between the demands of their parents with the demands of their peers could instill negative attitudes about schooling (Steinberg et al., 1992).
- *Parental Involvement.* In many source countries, the roles of parents and schools are sharply divided (Inger, 1992). Some parents are not accustomed to the parent-teacher interactive approach that many American school systems foster. Parents may believe that a teacher asking for their assistance at home with the child means that the teacher is incompetent. The teacher, however, assumes that the lack of enthusiasm to interact with the school on the parents' part is due to lack of interest in the child's schooling (Lareau, 1989).
- *The Need to Work to Support the Family.* Immigrant families tend to be poorer and larger than native families and the children are often expected to work to help support the family (McDonnell & Hill, 1993; Suárez-Orozco & Suárez -Orozco, 1995).
- *Mobility.* Immigrant parents, many of whom lack extensive schooling, may not be familiar with the demands of formal education and thus move their children to follow jobs or move back and forth from the country of origin. Many parents retain expectations for work and educational attainment derived from

their home cultures and so may not understand the need for high school graduation in the labor market of the United States (McDonnell & Hill, 1993; Pettit & McLanahan, 2003; Ream, 2003).

• *Psychological Adjustment.* Many immigrant children suffer from severe emotional stress, having endured family separations or possible violence in their home countries (Henderson, 1980; Thomas, 1992; McDonell & Hill, 1993).

In addition to the already forbidding array of obstacles listed above, many of the children of immigrant parents are English language learners and have greater difficulty in subject-related classes than students whose first language is English. One reason is that English learners face the double challenge of learning English while simultaneously learning content (Bennici & Strang, 1995). The Council of Chief State School Officers stated that immigrant children are more likely to be retained in grades and placed in low academic tracks on the basis of insufficient English language skills and low academic progress (Stewart, 1993). A large number of recent immigrant students are entering U.S. middle and high schools with little or no prior formal schooling and low literacy rates (Broeder, 1998). For these students to succeed in school, they must learn to read, write, understand, and speak English, develop academic literacy in English to make the transition to the labor force or into other educational programs, and become socialized into American society. Much of this occurs during adolescence, a time of major emotional, physical, and psychological change (Mace-Matluck et al., 1998). Beyond struggling with the content or psychological adjustments, school may be difficult for English language learners because "social language" (language used to converse with a friend or to complete routine tasks) and "academic language" (language used in subject-matter discussions and texts) can be quite different. Students may need five to nine years of instruction to acquire academic language, even if they seem proficient in social language (Cummins, 1996). In addition, science and math disciplines use specialized language, beyond the "academic language" (Crandall et al., 1985), and this can inhibit English language learners' understanding of certain concepts (Collier, 1992). Teachers of English language learners need to be sympathetic to different learning styles and frames of reference for learning, but they often are not (Kessler, 1987).

The difficulties in a classroom that English language learners encounter are most pronounced for Latino students. By the year 2010, Latinos are expected to be the largest minority group in the U.S., making up 21 percent of the population and having the highest rate of Limited English Proficient youth (Del Piñal & Garcia, 1994; Holman, 1997). According to Kaufman et al. (1998), about 18 percent of Latino children are born outside of the United States and 66 percent of Latino children come from a home where a language other than English is spoken. Statistics from *The Condition of Education 2003* show that in 1999, 14 percent of all students enrolled in grades K-12 were Latino students. Fifty-seven percent of Latino students in grades K-12 spoke mostly English at home, 25 percent spoke mostly Spanish, and 17 percent spoke English and Spanish equally. While 83 percent of Latino students who spoke mostly English at home had parents with a high school education or higher, this was true of only 49 percent of Latino students who spoke mostly Spanish at home (Wirt et al., 2000).

Youth from non-English-language backgrounds are 1.5 times more likely to leave school before high school graduation than those from English-language backgrounds (Driscoll, 1999; Secada et al., 1998). Though dropout rates have declined overall in recent years, especially among African-Americans and whites, the trend for Latino students is quite the opposite (Fernandez et al., 1989; Hugh, 1997). In 1992 roughly 50 percent of Latinos ages 16 to 24 dropped out of high school, and this number rose to about 60 percent in 1998 (Vaznaugh, 1995; Secada et al. 1998). This high dropout rate among Latino high school students is cause for growing concern because future earnings are linked to educational attainment. Providing appropriate instruction to immigrant students who are English language learners has become an issue of particular concern to educators across the country (Hurtado & Garcia, 1994).

YEARS OF SCHOOLING, POVERTY LEVELS, AND OCCUPATIONAL STATUS OF RECENT IMMIGRANTS

Further complicating the issue of geographic concentration of the growing number of immigrants' school-age children, immigrant parents may have fewer years of schooling and thus lower earnings than natives, so the tax contributions of immigrants are unlikely to offset the entire cost imposed on schools for educating these children. This is especially true because of the higher costs associated with teaching children whose first language is not English. Figure 1.3 charts the educational attainment of the native-born population and those born outside of the United States as of 2000. More native members of the population have received a basic education than foreign-born people. A little more than 30 percent of immigrants do not have a high school degree. In comparison, 7.6 percent of natives lack a high school education. However, attainment of a bachelor's degree or more is relatively equal for both natives and foreign-born: approximately 30 percent of both populations have a bachelor's degree or more.

Although it is apparent that a large portion of immigrants in the United States has not completed high school, educational attainment varies by country of origin. Figure 1.4 shows percentages of immigrants from a given source country who have less than a high school degree. Of the top ten sending countries, Spanish-speaking countries have the highest percentages of adults with less than a high school degree, ranging from 68 percent for Mexico to 22 percent for Colombia. Conversely, the Philippines, Russia, Korea, and India have the lowest proportion of non-high school graduates.

The high percentage of immigrants with less than a high school diploma may be a function of undocumented entrants, who are difficult to track and are often not the target of business-related immigration policy, which instead targets those with professional or graduate school degrees. Much research focuses on the effects of this relatively large number of "unskilled" immigrant workers on the wages and employment opportunities of native-born workers (Borjas, 1999; Borjas, 2000; Chiswick, 1977).

Figure 1.3: Educational Attainment of Immigrants and Natives

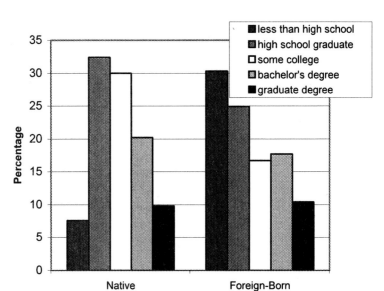

Note: Sample is adults aged 25 or over who are not enrolled in school

Sources: U.S. Census Bureau: 2002 Current Population Survey, Annual Social and Economic Data Supplement

According to the 1999 Current Population Survey, the poverty rate for immigrants is almost 50 percent higher than that of natives: 16.8 percent of the foreign-born and 11.2 percent of the native-born population lives below the poverty line (Schmidley, 2001).[2] Immigrants from different countries have different poverty rates, and differences in the poverty rates can be associated with differences in years of schooling (Jencks, 1972).

The high percentage of immigrants with less than a high school diploma may be a function of undocumented entrants, who are difficult to track and are often not the target of business-related immigration policy, which instead targets those with professional or graduate school degrees. Much research focuses on the effects of this relatively large number of "unskilled" immigrant workers on the wages and employment opportunities of native-born workers (Borjas, 1999; Borjas, 2000; Chiswick, 1977).

Figure 1.4: Percent of Immigrants with Less than a High School Diploma by Country of Origin

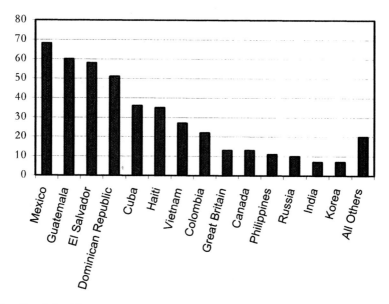

Note: Sample is adults aged 25 or over who are not enrolled in school
Source: U.S. Census Bureau: 2002 Current Population Survey, Annual Social and Economic Data Supplement

In 2002, the median earning of immigrants age 18 or over who held a full-time job for at least part of 2001 was only about 75 percent that of natives: $24,000 for immigrant workers compared with $31,200 for native workers. Although about 15 percent of the total work force is immigrant, they comprise 40.6 percent of the work force without a high school education (Camarota, 2002). Given the large proportion of immigrants with few years of schooling, it is not surprising that immigrants are relegated to low-status jobs and are significantly poorer as a group than are natives. Occupations that attract a higher proportion of immigrants are those that require less education.

In analyses of the 2002 Current Population Survey, Camarota (2002:9) finds a clear pattern to immigrant employment: those occupations that attract a higher proportion of immigrants are those that require less education. While immigrants make up only nine percent of individuals in managerial and professional jobs, they comprise 19 percent of those holding non-private service jobs, such as janitor, security guard or childcare worker. And, immigrants comprise a full 44 percent of those employed in private-sector service jobs, such as gardener or maid employed by an individual. Occupations filled predominantly with immigrants pay an average of only 60 percent of what occupations filled predominantly by native workers pay ($23,478 compared to $44,150).

STATUS ATTAINMENT PROCESSES WITHIN IMMIGRANT FAMILIES

These data draw a daunting picture of recently arriving immigrant adults in the United States: they tend to have lower educational attainment and higher poverty rates than native-born adults. In addition, they are concentrated in certain parts of the United States and in certain metropolitan areas, leading some to claim that they are straining local resources. The lower educational attainment of these immigrant adults could translate into the lower educational attainment for their children, as traditional status attainment models predict. The differences between the characteristics of immigrant and native-born adults in the workforce could certainly play a role in any differences in the schooling success of their children. Given the lower social status in which disproportionate numbers of immigrant families find themselves, one would expect the children growing up in these families to have lower levels of achievement. We need to ask if economically and socially comparable immigrant and native parents would have children with comparable educational attainment patterns. Is school success for children of immigrants directly associated with their parents' socioeconomic status before arriving to the United States? Or, do other factors such as the family's involvement in school or the youth's assimilation into mainstream American lifestyle affect how far they go in school?

Traditional status attainment models that connect the occupation and education of parents to their child's subsequent education often neglect the unique position of immigrants in the United States. Blau & Duncan's (1967) landmark research on status attainment patterns did include some consideration of social mobility patterns for white ethnic immigrants. Since this study, the Family Reunification Act of 1965 has brought a much different immigrant population to the borders of this country; most immigrants arriving after 1965 are now from Asia, the Caribbean, and Latin America and have a very different profile from that of previous immigrant groups (Betts & Lofstrom, 1998). More recent approaches have attempted to broaden the scope of the traditional status attainment model by investigating black-white differences (Gottfredson, 1981); gender differences (Sewell, Hauser & Wolf, 1980); and even differences between the effect of mother's or father's education and occupation (Sewell, Hauser & Featherman, 1976). Present research that does examine intergenerational status attainment of immigrants and their children focuses either on differences in wages and earnings or on educational attainment; it does not consider parents' socioeconomic status prior to arriving in the United States—a methodological weakness that this study ameliorates. Because of potential lack of opportunities faced by immigrant adults, coupled with the geographic concentration of the recently arriving immigrant population, I suggest that this straight-line status attainment process may not operate for all immigrant households. Below, I summarize the recent literature on intergenerational status attainment for immigrants and their children and offer suggestions for improvement.

Intergenerational Analyses Using Earnings

The examination of differences in wages between immigrant generations is one method to examine the intergenerational transmission of status. The children of immigrants who arrived in the post-1965 wave have not been in the labor market for enough years to enable the collection of detailed data. Therefore, this topic has not been as vastly explored as differences in mean wages between native and immigrant adult workers (e.g., Altonji & Card, 1991) or differences in educational attainment among different cohorts of immigrants.

The use of earnings or wages enables researchers to study tangible returns to education and how differences in returns compare across cohorts or between generations. Two of the first studies of mean earnings differences between immigrant generations were by Chiswick (1977) and Carliner (1980). These studies used cross-sectional data from the 1970 Census to calculate the relative wages of various generations of Americans. Both Chiswick and Carliner find that the mean wages of second-generation immigrants converged with, and even exceeded, the mean wage of the first-generation workers, but that the mean wages of the third generation did not achieve parity with the second generation's earnings and even dropped below.

More recent work by Borjas (1992; 1993; 1994) improved previous studies by using longitudinal data to analyze differences in earnings. Using 1970 and 1990 Census data, he found that the rate of intergenerational mobility between immigrants and their children is influenced not only by parental background, but also by the "quality" of the ethnic environment where the children grow up. The notion of "ethnic capital," based in part on Coleman's (1988) concept of social capital, is that "the average human capital stock in the parental generation for ethnic groups acts as an externality in the production of the human capital of children" (Borjas, 1994: 1712).

Although this work adds immeasurably to our understanding of how immigrant cohorts differ from each other, cohort analyses of census data do not enable one to examine the intergenerational status attainment process from parent to child within a single family. I expand on the ideas developed within this body of research and frame my analyses around the intergenerational status attainment within a family in order to understand not only what happens through time with immigrants, but also how status is transferred from immigrant parent to child.

This present study also augments previous work by including two population groups (self-employed workers and employed women) and a measure of economic performance (the prestige of an occupation), which are often omitted in analyses. First, by not including self-employed workers, an entire group of immigrants (small business owners or merchants for example) is excluded—and many immigrants take this route to success. These people may be relatively high income-earners, but are not counted in the work of economists who want to calculate "labor income" and who see income from self-employment partly as a return to capital, rather than as a return to labor. Second, the comparison of mean wages to determine intergenerational transmission of status invariably focuses on male adult wage earners. By focusing on males, these studies exclude what women contribute to a family's income. Third, some jobs may not yield a high income, but may garner a relatively high status for a particular immigrant group. A perception of status, based on the occupation rather than on income alone, could have positive outcomes for the immigrant's offspring because of the perceptions and expectations for educational attainment. The data used in this study allow me to incorporate all employed people in my study; I also account for small business owners as well as women, all of whom may influence the shape of the status attainment patterns for both the first and subsequent generations. By looking at occupation in addition to earnings, this study provides a broader picture of the patterns of intergenerational status attainment of immigrants.

Intergenerational Analyses Using Educational Attainment

As mentioned earlier, there is a large body of literature that examines differences in education attainments among immigrant generations. Some studies claim that first-generation students—those that were born abroad and started their schooling in the U.S. after first grade—do better in school and go farther in school than succeeding generations (Ogbu, 1991; Suárez-Orozco & Suárez-Orozco, 1995; Portes & Rumbaut, 1996). Other studies find opposite results: first-generation students do worse than succeeding generations (Fligstein & Fernandez, 1985; Matute-Bianchi, 1986; Frenandez & Paulsen, 1989; Rong & Grant, 1992; Wojtkiewicz & Donato, 1995).

To explain why one generation (immigrant adults as compared to their second- or first-generation children) may be performing better in school or in the labor market than another, researchers have turned to assimilation theories. One theory is that immigrants positively self-select out of a country, and are thus predisposed to achieving academically. This perspective focuses on the circumstances that produce geographic movement and the selectivity of migrants. Chiswick (1986), Borjas (1990), and Ogbu (1991) are among recent researchers who propose the positive self-selection model to explain scholastic achievement of the first generation of immigrants. These authors argue that immigrants are predisposed to adapt to the host society. Although immigrants find themselves at the bottom of the socioeconomic ladder initially, they generally expect that they or their offspring will eventually experience upward mobility.

Ogbu (1991), for example, claims that voluntary immigrants tend to overcome difficulties experienced in their host country because their cultural frame of reference is their home country, where they often faced harsher environments than they do in the U.S. Also, because voluntary immigrants view their adjustment problems as temporary, they are more creative in inventing pragmatic solutions to their current predicaments. By contrast, many minorities who have lived in the United States for several generations are disillusioned with the prospects of upward mobility because of their experiences with discrimination (Waters, 2001). This positive self-selection theory, however, may be a more appropriate device for "economic" immigrants than for political refugees, whose migration to the United States involves a wide variety of people from all parts of the social strata of a source country. In addition, this model may only be applicable to the situation of immigrants whose income and educational distribution is similar to that found in the United States (Borjas, 1994).

Another theory is the straight-line assimilation framework. This model predicts that over time ethnic and racial minorities will blend into the mainstream culture and become indistinguishable from native populations (Park, 1914; Gordon, 1964). This is a multi-staged process by which the immigrant comes into contact with the mainstream society and slowly integrates. Often, language ability becomes a marker of assimilation. Matute-Bianchi's (1986) study of a California high school lends support to the straight-line assimilation hypothesis. She found that the most successful students within the Mexican population she studied usually spoke English exclusively in school and participated in mainstream clubs rather than those geared toward Mexican students.

Although Matute-Bianchi finds that assimilation improves educational outcomes for the group she studied, this classic assimilation model does not offer an explanation for Mexican Americans' lack of intergenerational social and economic mobility, despite their rapid attitudinal assimilation (Portes & Zhou, 1993). Some researchers even suggest that the greater assimilation of Mexican Americans to the United States' cultural life has been the major reason for their inability to succeed (Suárez-Orozco & Suárez-Orozco, 1995).

To explain why some children of immigrants students do less well in school the more adapted they become to U.S. culture, some argue that foreign-born youth are especially motivated to succeed academically and thus may be the highest academic achievers (Gibson, 1988; Rumbaut & Ima, 1988; Caplan, et al., 1991; Duran, 1992). This theory of assimilation—accommodation without assimilation—posits that academic achievement declines in time as immigrant youth assimilate with their native peers. Gibson (1988), for example, found that Punjabi children of immigrants excelled much more than their foreign-born ethnic counterparts because they did not fully assimilate into the mainstream peer culture. They retained tight connections to the values of their immigrant parents and so had high levels of academic performance and attainment. This theory suggests that strong co-ethnic communities that have the social and economic resources to reinforce the parental culture will bring about better student success. Thus, rapid assimilation brings about disastrous consequences (Suárez-Orozco, 1987; Suárez-Orozco, 1989). The most academically successful students are those who remain most closely allied with the culture of their parents because of group resources and attitudes: the group "accommodates" the culture of the U.S. "without assimilation."

In contrast to the above theories, a fourth model, segmented assimilation, does not claim higher or lower academic performance or educational attainment for any particular generation. Instead, each immigrant group's experiences differ according to the "mode of incorporation" into a host society (Portes & Böröcz, 1991). The theory of segmented assimilation helps to explain the role geographic concentration has in determining the educational attainment of children. Segmented assimilation posits that the type of community in which the immigrant group lives determines the social and economic assimilation patterns of the individuals and the group as a whole (Rumbaut, 1994). Distinct forms of adaptation emerge from the acculturation and assimilation of an immigrant group into a specific social and economic sector of American society, which in turn shapes intergenerational mobility (Portes & Zhou, 1993; Portes & Rumbaut, 1996). According to this model, an immigrant group from Mexico, for example, has lower educational attainment due to realistic appraisals of the relatively lower return to educational investment in the United States for their ethnic group (Suárez-Orozco & Suárez-Orozco, 1995; Portes & Zhou, 1993; Kao & Tienda, 1995). This results in an adversarial stance common among impoverished groups confined to the bottom of the economic hourglass (Suárez-Orozco & Suárez-Orozco, 1995).

These theories of assimilation provide a strong foundation for understanding the underpinnings of scholastic success for children in immigrant households. However, as mentioned earlier, this body of literature remains ambiguous about which generation does better in school for three methodological reasons.

First, it uses cross-sectional quantitative and qualitative studies to estimate what are essentially longitudinal patterns. To elaborate on this, consider that statistical analyses of large data sets tend to be cross-sectional, employing statistical models using only one year of a data set (Rong & Grant, 1992; Portes & Zhou, 1993; Kao & Tienda, 1995; Zsembik & Llanes, 1996). Furthermore, these studies do not compare parents and children from the same family, preventing the researchers from looking at intergenerational "mobility," although claiming to do so. They define "first-generation" as students who are born outside of the United States and "subsequent generations" by whether the native-born students' parents are born outside of the United States. Thus, comments about social mobility patterns based on how well the "first generation" does compared to "subsequent generations" are misleading because those in the second generation are not, in fact, the descendants of the first generation. Instead, these are two sets of children of the same age observed in the same year, who are encountering similar historical circumstances to their schooling success. Intergenerational analyses should take into consideration the timing differences in the two generations' arrival to the United States. The longitudinal nature of my analyses allows me to address this problem by including a specific generational analysis that compares children's academic success based upon the characteristics of their parents.

Adding to the problem that most quantitative work on this topic is cross-sectional is the fact that most work on immigrant students is qualitative and thus analyzes educational and mobility patterns one immigrant community at a time (e.g., Gibson, 1988; Caplan et al., 1991; Portes & Zhou, 1993; Waters, 1997). It is valuable to have ethnographic research that focuses on a particular group or groups because each community has different needs and a different mix of ethnic and language minority students entering their school systems. Much of the research on ethnic group differences in achievement, such as Gibson (1988), Rumberger & Larson (1998), or Delgado-Gaitan &

Trueba (1991), has focused on a single ethnic group. Differences in the educational experiences of students can be attributed to differences in their families and their school experiences, rather than to differences in the types of schools they attend or the communities in which they live (see Portes & MacLeod, 1996, for such arguments, and Rumberger & Larson, 1998: 75-76). These qualitative studies provide important hypotheses about immigrant scholastic and labor market success based on assimilation patterns, but cannot be generalized beyond the individual populations examined.

Recent work combines qualitative and quantitative methods to compare practices that appear successful in raising achievement levels of minority and limited English proficient students at the district level (Dentler & Hafner, 1997). However, a multiple-case comparison is limited in its ability to identify explanations for the pattern of differences between observed behaviors and documented events. Such a design cannot test causal hypotheses. This is especially so when the comparisons are grounded in one-time site visits, even when these include collection of historical trends. Comparative case analysis does permit the researcher to eliminate hypotheses. It can also point toward practices that have greater empirical credence as sources of success in fostering achievement. However, this methodological approach does not enable researchers to compare across-group differences. The study in this book alleviates these two methodological problems by employing a national data set with sufficient numbers of students that are directly compared with their parents.

Second, researchers of immigration and education do not use pre-arrival information when measuring a family's socioeconomic status. Instead, these studies use a composite measure of parents' education (potentially received in the United States), occupation and tangible possessions in the home (e.g., Fligstein & Fernandez, 1985; Kao & Tienda, 1995). By not including pre-arrival information, the researchers omit half of the information relevant to the status of the parents. For a number of reasons, recent immigrants hold a unique position in the U.S. labor market that may cause their social mobility patterns to differ from the patterns of the native-born population. For example, often immigrant adults enter a segmented labor market; they are either highly skilled with high educational attainment, or are low-skilled and have only a small amount of formal schooling. In addition, there could be a discrepancy between post-arrival occupation and the immigrant adult's true skills and educational attainment. Often, immigrants take low-skilled jobs that do not correspond with their educational attainment because their degrees may not be recognized in the United States. The analyses in this study specifically measure the relative effects of pre-arrival education and the post-arrival social status of the immigrant adults.

Third, current research suffers from a lack of statistical analyses that test hypotheses of how assimilation into immigrant neighborhoods can affect the connection between a parent's and child's social status, a vital component of the segmented assimilation theory. The theory of segmented assimilation seems to be able to explain the variety of assimilation patterns for students and adults of different ethnicities. Unfortunately, much of the research that claims to test segmented assimilation fails to delve deeply into the characteristics of the community into which the immigrant adult or child assimilates. Instead, researchers claim to uphold the theory of segmented assimilation whenever a racial or ethnic effect in regression analyses on a child's academic achievement or educational attainment remains after controlling for parents' educational attainment (see, for example, Portes & MacLeod, 1996; Kao & Tienda, 1995 or Hao & Bornstead, 1998).[3]

The theory of segmented assimilation is a valuable contribution to understanding the patterns of assimilation of immigrant adults and children. Therefore, a closer look at the components of the community into which the immigrant adult or child is assimilating is needed in order to fully test this theory. Measuring the effects of an immigrant adult or child living in a community with a concentration of people who are foreigners or of the same ethnicity can provide us with that test.

I address these three problems in previous research by conducting a longitudinal analysis of a national data set; constructing an appropriate variable of socioeconomic status that includes a variety of measures of family background; and including the social and economic context of the community where the student attends school.

THE EFFECTS OF COMMUNITY CONTEXT ON CHILD'S EDUCATIONAL ATTAINMENT

Whether the concentration of an immigrant community serves as a springboard for economic advancement or as a trap into a spiral of downward mobility is determined in part by the social capital and ethnic capital of that community. According to James Coleman (1994), social capital "...inheres in the structure of relations between persons and among persons. ...The function identified by the concept 'social capital' is the value of those aspects of social structure to actors, as resources that can be used by the actors to realize their interests" (302, 305). The essence is a "dense set of associations" within a social group promoting cooperative behavior that is advantageous to group members. Social capital appears not simply in the individual, but in the structure of social organizations, patterns of social relationships, and the processes of interactions among individuals and organizations.

Social capital has two basic functions, applicable in a variety of contexts: as a source of social control and as a source of benefits through extra-familial networks (Portes, 1998). A close-knit community, measured in terms of the proximity of other immigrants or of co-ethnic peers, could negatively or positively affect a child's schooling outcomes depending on these two functions of social capital. First, having fellow immigrants or co-ethnic peers could be beneficial because of the social control developed and ensured by close ties of family members with other community members. Zhou & Bankston (1994) exemplify this form of social capital as social control in their study of Vietnamese in New Orleans—in which "both parents and children are constantly observed as under a 'Vietnamese microscope'" (207). The source of this type of social capital is found in bounded solidarity and enforceable trust, and its main result is to render formal or overt controls unnecessary (Portes, 1998). The second, and most common function attributed to social capital, is as a source of network-mediated benefits beyond the immediate family, which enhances access to employment, mobility through occupational ladders, and entrepreneurial success (Portes, 1998). Granovetter (1974), for example, coined the term "strength of weak ties" to refer to the power of indirect influences outside the immediate circle of family and close friends to serve as an informal employment referral system.

Social capital, as social control, family connections, or networking opportunities, is often perceived as a positive influence in the educational or economic life of a person. However, social capital has a potential "dark side" (Fiorina, 1999; Putnam, 2000). Strong community ties could be detrimental to the occupational success of the immigrant adults in the community because the lack of occupational or language opportunities may have a negative impact on the academic potential of their children. Another term for this is "institutional completeness," which refers to the extent to which an immigrant ethnic group can meet the needs of its members (Breton, 1964). If an ethnic group can meet those needs, then its members will have little contact with non-group members. In addition, close ties within a group will not provide much of an advantage for the schooling of the children if group members do not hold much "capital" or resources to share.

The second theory that can help us understand how the community affects the intergenerational transmission of status for children in immigrant households is ethnic capital (Borjas, 1994). Derived from the theory of social capital, ethnic capital refers to "the characteristics of the ethnic environment such as the skills and economic opportunities that permeate the ethnic networks" (Borjas, 2000:14). In line with much of the present literature on neighborhood effects, we can think of this concept in terms of availability of role models specific to that immigrant and ethnic group. According to the logic of this theory, immigrants who originate in countries that have abundant human capital and higher levels of per capita income tend to do better in the United States. Ethnic skill differentials may persist for at least three generations.

Borjas explains that those immigrants with lower education levels or literacy rates have children with lower educational attainment and lower wages. The economic impact of immigration obviously depends not only on how immigrants adapt, but also on the adjustment process experienced by their offspring. Borjas turns to the characteristics of the ethnic environment, the ethnic capital, in immigrant communities to explain why economic disparities would persist through generations. He surmises that the characteristics of the ethnic environment influence the skills and economic performance of the children in the ethnic group, above and beyond the influence of the parents. These characteristics include the culture, attitudes, and economic opportunities that permeate the ethnic networks. Exposure to an advantaged ethnic environment—in the sense that the environment has abundant human capital—has a positive influence on the children in the group, while exposure to a disadvantaged environment has a negative influence. Because few people in disadvantaged ethnic groups can afford to escape the ethnic ghetto, these enclaves make it easy for ethnic capital to influence the social mobility of individuals who reside there and help to perpetuate the socioeconomic differences observed across ethnic groups from generation to generation. Ethnic enclaves provide the social and economic networks that will influence the lives of the children and grandchildren of these immigrants far into the next century.

Greater social capital and potential ethnic capital in a student's community should positively affect children's educational attainment, even after considering parents' socioeconomic status. Conversely, offspring of disadvantaged immigrants would be expected to be caught in the double bind of slower socioeconomic mobility because of the family's living in an area with low community-level human capital (ethnic capital) and weaker personal and community bonds (social capital).

ORGANIZATION OF THE BOOK

Chapter Two looks at the roles of country of origin mean educational attainment and pre-arrival educational attainment of immigrant parents on the family's post-arrival occupational status (Part I of Figure 1.1). Chapter Three examines the role of the composition of the school population in which the student attends and the parents' social status on the child's educational attainment (Parts II and III of Figure 1.1). Chapter Four investigates the role of parental involvement in a child's schooling to probe the dilemma presented in Chapter Three: differences in educational attainment remain for children in native and immigrant families as well as for Puerto Rican, Mexican, Filipino, and Chinese students, even when controlling for family background, assimilation factors, and the density of the ties in the community. I conclude in Chapter Five with a summary of the findings, policy implications of this research, and avenues for future research.

CHAPTER 2

Predictors of Social Status: Investigating the Roles of Educational Attainment and Country of Origin

INTRODUCTION

It is difficult to ascertain whether the pre-arrival socioeconomic status of the immigrant adults determines their child's potential status attainment patterns more than the family's post-arrival social and economic status. One reason for this may be that immigrant adults are disproportionately found in the highest and the lowest socioeconomic brackets. In addition, where these immigrants were positioned in the educational and occupational attainment market in their country of origin could impact their future socioeconomic status in the United States. For example, immigrant adults with a high education level, and thus potentially high occupational status in their country of origin, may be able to obtain a high status occupation once in the United States. This would result in a higher income for the family, residence in a neighborhood with a stronger school district, and thus potentially greater learning and educational attainment for their children. However, an immigrant adult's occupation or education before coming to the United States may not tell us what type of occupation or earnings he or she will have once in the United States. Education and occupation from another country are often not directly translated into the same education level or occupation in the United States. For example, adults with a high occupational status who are not able to directly translate their education or occupation to a high occupational status in the United States would not be able to provide the same resources for learning to their children.

I hypothesize that neither the pre-arrival economic and social status information of the immigrant parents nor the post-arrival occupation of the parents, standing alone, will give us the complete picture of how well a child will do in school. Instead, both are important determinants of a child's educational attainment.

This chapter explores how educational attainment translates to occupation status for immigrant and native-born adults. Parental education is a key variable in social mobility studies (e.g., Haller & Portes, 1973; Spenner & Featherman, 1978) and current sociological studies use parental education and occupation in combination with other variables, such as income and tangible possessions in the home, to develop a measure of a person's socio-economic status in society. The aim is to fill the gaps in previous status attainment research on immigrants by examining how immigrant parents' experiences in the labor market of their country of origin help to explain their experiences in the labor market in the United States. Chapter Three takes this analysis one step further by examining how the social context of the immigrant family mediates the relationship between pre-arrival education and post-arrival social status, and how pre-arrival and post-arrival social status of the immigrant adults affect their children's schooling experiences.

In this chapter, I use data from the 1990 Public Use Micro-Sample of the U.S. Census to investigate the links between educational attainment and occupation for foreign-born and native-born adults in the United States between the ages of 28 and 55.[1] As one would expect, educational attainment is a clear predictor of occupational status for all the adults in the sample, especially for those populations born in the United States. Yet, this positive association is not consistent among all ethnic groups or for all immigrants, highlighting the importance to consider the social context in which the adults live as a determinant of their occupational chances and choices.

OCCUPATIONAL OPPORTUNITIES FOR IMMIGRANTS IN THE WORKFORCE

Adult immigrants have labor market experiences that differ from their native-born peers, experiences that could differentially affect the status attainment patterns of their children. Consistently, research finds that immigrant earnings differ by country of origin and time spent in the U.S., even when controlling for education and experience (Hendricks, 2001). One example, touched upon in the previous chapter, is that the educational attainment of immigrants as a whole is bifurcated compared to the native-born: either they are highly skilled with many years of schooling, or are low-skilled and have only a small amount of formal schooling. In addition, because immigrants are clustered geographically and often employed in the same jobs together (Bartel, 1989; LaLonde & Topel, 1991), they enter a more constrained labor market than their native-born peers and thus do not have many occupational choices (Perlmann & Waldinger, 1996). Another factor affecting the placement of an immigrant in the U.S. labor market is his or her English ability or "language capital" (Borjas, 1994); a good command of English expands job opportunities. Language proficiency, in turn, affects how well an immigrant student does in school and the education level attained (White, 1997; White & Kaufman, 1997; Mauw & Xie, 1999).[2] Relative perception of status attainment for immigrant and native-born workers can also be a factor. For example, an immigrant may have a stronger sense of self worth than a native worker with the same years of schooling because the latter compares himself to the general educated population in the United States. As a result, the immigrant may not limit him or herself to only those jobs that a native-born worker would consider.

One of the most important reasons why status attainment patterns within immigrant families may differ from those within native-born families is that some immigrants often have little choice but to take low-skilled jobs that do not correspond with their educational attainment. Their credentials may not be recognized in the United States, resulting in "status inconsistency," discussed below. Three occupational trajectories for immigrant adults in the United States labor market exist. One, they acquire the same type of job that their skill levels demand. This could occur for highly-trained and highly-educated workers who are recruited to come to the United States on an HB-1 (business) visa. A well-known example of this trajectory type is nurses from the West Indies. Jamaican women, in particular, are recruited by top hospitals around the United States upon graduation from nursing schools because of a severe shortage of nurses in the United States. Another example is Silicon Valley software developers from India. Alternatively, the worker is low-skilled and has few years of education and has a menial job in the United States that is consistent with the job (or lack thereof) they would have had in the country of origin. One clear example of this trajectory is manual-labor workers (predominantly undocumented) who must find work in the private service sector as gardeners, maids, or housekeepers.

A second occupational trajectory is one in which there is an appreciable rise in the adult's occupational status or earnings. This could happen to workers who immigrated for economic opportunity and were able to acquire a job that provides them with a greater income and occupational status than any job they could have in the country of origin. This is usually the hope of many economic immigrants. An example of this would be a Vietnamese store owner who has very few years of education, but is able to buy a store with the assistance of loans taken from his fellow Vietnamese. He is thus able to earn a much larger income than his education would have garnered in Vietnam and secure an occupation and income that are not education dependent.

A third occupational trajectory is a downward shift in occupational status. Often, professional degrees from another country are not recognized in the United States and the engineer, teacher, medical doctor, lawyer or other professional must obtain a job for which his or her years of education would normally make him or her overqualified. These immigrants may choose to remain in the United States because they are either political refugees and thus cannot return home or because they feel that their children will have better educational and labor force opportunities in the United States.

This chapter explores these occupational trajectories for immigrant adults in the labor market to understand how the educational attainment of adults before coming to the United States affects their occupational status once in the United States.

DATA AND VARIABLES

Data for the analyses in this chapter are drawn from the 1990 5-percent Public Use Micro Samples of the U.S. Census (5% PUMS) and the International Data on Educational Attainment (2000). Respondents in the sample are between the ages of 28 and 55, and I select only those immigrant adults who arrived in the United States after age 23. The dependent variable is a measure of occupational status in the United States based on the 1988 socioeconomic index (SEI) scores administrators for the National Education Longitudinal Study use. Because I use the NELS data set to examine the educational attainment of children of immigrant and native adults in subsequent chapters, I use the NELS categorization of SEI to maintain consistency among the analyses. Table 2.1 lists the occupation and respective SEI coding.

Table 2.1: Socio-Economic Index Occupational Codes

Occupation	SEI Code
Laborer	29.44
Service sector	30.46
Operative/machinist	34.10
Farmer/farm manager	35.57
Sales	35.77
Clerical	38.16
Craftsperson	38.51
Protective services	48.40
Proprietor/ owner	50.64
Technical	51.21
Manager/ administration	53.52
"Professionals" such as nurse, accountant, dentist, lawyer, doctor, school teacher	64.38

The classification of occupations constitutes the backbone of much, if not most, stratification research: "Ever since it was recognized that the division of labor is the kernel of social inequality and occupation therefore is the main dimension of social stratification, stratification researchers have developed ways to derive status measures from information on occupations" (Gazenboom & Treiman,

1996: 202). SEI scales are more widely used by stratification researchers than are prestige scales or ordinal class categorizations because they capture the basic parameters of the process of stratification somewhat better (Featherman & Hauser, 1976).

I measure educational attainment with years of schooling. Since I select foreign-born adults who arrived in the United States after age 23, schooling has most likely been completed by time of arrival. Thus, for foreign-born adults, the level of education is a measure of pre-arrival education (except for those immigrants who arrive after age 23 who may have attended graduate school in the United States).[3] Other independent variables I use to examine the relationship between education and social status are age, gender, English ability, and length of time in the United States (if the person is an immigrant). Length of time in the United States is a dummy variable coded 1 for those respondents who arrived within the last five years, zero for all others. English ability is a five-point scale based on a self-determined ranking of the respondent's ability to speak English. (5: Speaks only English; 4: Speaks English very well; 3: Speaks English well; 2: Speaks English "not well"; 1: Speaks English "not at all").

I measure the country of origin human capital of immigrant adults with mean years of schooling in the country of origin from the International Data on Educational Attainment data set, which has data on the mean years of schooling for both men and women over the age of twenty-five from 163 countries from 1960-1999. I control for the country-level human capital alongside the individual-level human capital of the immigrant adults to test if the evidence presented in Chapter One of declining education level of recent cohorts of immigrants—whether due to the changes in current source countries' level of development (Borjas, 2001) or to changes in the type of immigrant who arrives (Camarota, 2002)—affects the post-arrival status attainment of the family. I match country-level mean years of schooling to each immigrant adult based on his or her gender for 1999. (If the adult is native-born, I use the mean years of schooling in the United States.) To remain consistent with analyses that use the National Education Longitudinal Study in subsequent chapters, I categorize the countries in the International Data on Educational Attainment by region or country of origin according to the ethnic categories in the NELS data set. For example, to determine the mean levels of education for the countries of origin of "white" immigrants, I use the numbers for

Canada and Australia, as well as Northern and Western European countries. Estimates for Puerto Rico and Cuba are not available from the International Data on Educational Attainment. I calculate these mean years of schooling from data published by each island's Ministry of Education. Appendix A tabulates the mean years of schooling by gender for all countries available in the data set that I use in the regional estimates presented in the next section.

MEAN YEARS OF EDUCATION FOR IMMIGRANTS FOR COUNTRY OF ORIGIN AND RACE/ETHNICITY

Table 2.2 shows the mean years of schooling for foreign-born and native-born males and females in the United Stats by country of origin. The last three columns show the mean level of schooling for each country or region. Several interesting patterns emerge from the table:

- When we compare the mean educational attainment at the country or regional level with that of immigrants who currently live in the United States, we see a drastic difference between the mean levels of educational attainment for foreign-born population in the United States and the mean levels of education in their countries of origin: the mean levels of education for the foreign-born in the United States is well above the mean education level of their countries of origin. Evidently, the people entering the United States from overseas are not the least educated from their origin countries. Instead, most immigrants are fairly well educated relative to the mean level of education in their countries of origin.[4]
- Regardless of race/ethnicity, females have lower educational attainment than males overall.
- Mean educational averages for immigrant and natives differ greatly by country of origin or ethnicity, except for whites and Japanese, whose mean years of education for natives and immigrants are fairly similar. For most other ethnic groups, foreigners on average have fewer years of schooling than their native counterparts. However, the larger standard deviations for mean years of schooling for foreigners compared to natives show that there is greater variation in educational attainment

Table 2.2: Mean Levels of Schooling by Country and Gender

	Foreign-Born			Native-Born			Country/Region of Origin		
	Male	Female	Average	Male	Female	Average	Male	Female	Average
Northern & Western European (White)	13.48	12.87	13.19	13.50	13.34	13.42	9.57	8.85	9.20
	(3.90)	(3.74)	(3.84)	(2.73)	(2.47)	(2.60)			
African & Afro-Caribbean (Black)	15.23	12.57	13.89	12.22	12.80	12.53	4.13	3.09	3.60
	(3.29)	(3.78)	(3.78)	(2.61)	(2.49)	(2.57)			
Mexican	7.60	5.81	6.93	11.93	11.93	11.93	7.16	6.32	6.73
	(4.98)	(4.60)	(4.92)	(3.63)	(4.07)	(3.85)			
Puerto Rican	10.59	8.54	9.10	12.39	13.51	12.88	N/A	N/A	7.00
	(4.27)	(3.35)	(3.73)	(1.69)	(1.68)	(1.77)			
Cuban	10.32	10.59	10.45	13.99	17.14	15.57	N/A	N/A	7.23
	(4.51)	(4.05)	(4.29)	(1.39)	(2.15)	(2.41)			
Latin & South American (other Latino)	11.09	9.93	10.64	12.53	12.36	12.44	5.91	5.78	5.84
	(3.86)	(3.91)	(3.92)	(3.01)	(2.89)	(2.95)			
Chinese	13.86	11.93	12.87	17.11	15.21	16.64	8.78	7.00	7.91
	(4.82)	(5.32)	(5.17)	(1.84)	(1.92)	(2.03)			
Filipino	14.44	14.31	14.36	13.04	13.03	13.03	7.54	7.69	7.62
	(2.91)	(3.02)	(2.97)	(2.83)	(2.06)	(2.47)			
Korean	15.28	12.49	14.21	13.43	13.69	15.68	11.54	9.42	10.46
	(2.53)	(3.80)	(3.36)	(3.60)	(3.71)	(2.36)			

(continued on next page)

Table 2.2: (continued)

	Foreign-Born			Native-Born			Country/Region of Origin		
	Male	Female	Average	Male	Female	Average	Male	Female	Average
Japanese	15.19	13.50	14.20	16.19	14.69	13.56	10.13	9.34	9.72
	(3.26)	(2.85)	(3.13)	(2.86)	(1.95)	(3.62)			
South Asian	16.58	14.22	15.25	14.76	13.55	12.88	4.89	2.94	3.94
	(2.85)	(3.88)	(3.66)	(2.97)	(2.95)	(2.62)			
South East Asian	12.38	12.54	12.46	12.71	13.50	14.12	4.59	3.97	4.27
	(4.08)	(5.17)	(4.66)	(2.62)	(3.53)	(3.01)			
Pacific Islander	11.59	11.28	11.44	12.86	12.73	12.80	5.60	4.74	5.18
	(3.94)	(2.80)	(3.41)	(2.19)	(2.39)	(2.29)			
Other Asian/ Other Ethnicity	14.12	12.57	13.77	14.36	14.09	14.18	6.10	4.48	5.30
	(2.21)	(4.44)	(2.93)	(2.70)	(1.55)	(2.00)			
TOTAL (United States)	12.09	11.05	11.62	13.31	13.24	13.27	12.29	12.21	12.25
	(4.91)	(4.96)	(4.96)	(2.79)	(2.53)	(2.66)			

Sources: Individual-level data from the 5% Public Use Micro-Samples of the 1990 U.S. Census; country-level indicators from the International Data on Educational Attainment (2000)

Note: Sample includes adults age 25 and older; foreign-born adults arrived in the U.S. at age 23 or older

N/A: Not Available

for foreigners. Filipinos and South Asian are exceptions: Filipinos and South Asians born in the U.S. have, on average, fewer years of schooling than immigrant Filipinos and South Asians.

As shown in Appendix A, some of the lowest estimates of average years of schooling are those for African and Afro-Caribbean countries (3.60 average years) and for India, Pakistan, and Bangladesh (3.94 average years)—marked as South Asian in Table 2.2. Japan, Korea, and the European countries that comprise the "White" category are among the countries with a relatively high mean educational attainment—figures that are consistent with other measures of a country's development, such as gross domestic product or purchasing power parity.

RELATIONSHIP BETWEEN OCCUPATIONAL STATUS AND EDUCATIONAL ATTAINMENT

The next set of tables briefly touches on the strength and direction of relationships between the dependent and independent variables in my model, as measured by the correlation coefficients (Table 2.3). The first matrix shows the associations for all respondents in the sample. The second selects native-born adults; the third, foreign-born adults who arrived in the United States at age 23 or older. As one would expect, adults' educational attainment is positively correlated with occupational status in all three matrices in Table 2.3 (r =.512 for all respondents; r =.525 for native respondents; r =.496 for foreign respondents). Another positive, albeit weak, relationship exists in the correlation matrix for all respondents between years of education and English ability (r =.252): the more years of education, the greater the respondent's command of English.

Table 2.3: Correlation Matrices of Independent and Dependent Variables

All Respondents

N = 486,058	1	2	3	4	5	6	7	8
1. Occupation Status	1.000							
2. Years of Education	.512	1.000						
3. Country Mean Education	.010	.126	1.000					
4. Arrived within Five Years	.014	-.075	-.543	1.000				
5. Age	.016	-.114	-.016	-.062	1.000			
6. English Ability	.101	.252	.593	-.405	-.045	1.000		
7. Female	.050	-.015	-.016	-.034	-.014	.028	1.000	
8. Foreign	-.017	-.133	-.939	.592	.033	-.663	-.036	1.000

Native-Born Respondents

N = 462,108	1	2	3	4	5	6	7	8
1. Occupation Status	1.000							
2. Years of Education	.525	1.000						
3. Country Mean Education	-.056	.012	1.000					
4. Arrived within Five Years	N/A	N/A	N/A	N/A				
5. Age	.025	-.116	.015	N/A	1.000			
6. English Ability	.048	.087	-.020	N/A	-.022	1.000		
7. Female	.056	-.012	-1.000	N/A	-.015	.020	1.000	
8. Foreign	N/A	N/A	N/A	N/A	N/A	N/A	N/A	N/A

Foreign-Born Respondents

N = 24,150	1	2	3	4	5	6	7	8
1. Occupation Status	1.000							
2. Years of Education	.496	1.000						
3. Country Mean Education	-.113	-.034	1.000					
4. Arrived within Five Years	-.071	-.062	.119	1.000				
5. Age	-.153	-.079	.174	.580	1.000			
6. English Ability	.506	.574	-.139	-.158	-.102	1.000		
7. Female	-.056	-.104	-.214	-.049	.018	-.054	1.000	
8. Foreign	N/A	N/A	N/A	N/A	N/A	N/A	N/A	N/A

Source: 5% Public Use Micro-Sample of the 1990 U.S. Census
Sample: all adults age 28-55; foreign-born adults arrived to the U.S. after age 23
N/A: Not Applicable

Being foreign-born, however, is not strongly associated with one's English ability (r =-.133), suggesting that being foreign does not necessarily mean that you will not know English well. For foreign-born respondents, English ability has a positive relationship with occupational status (r =.506)—similar to the association between education and occupation (r =.496). Additionally, English ability has a positive association with one's education (r =.576). It is thus clear that one's English ability is related to one's education level and that an increase in either of these variables will bring about a rise in one's occupational standing.

These correlation matrices offer a glimpse into which variables are associated with others, but they do not answer the question of how these variables operate together to affect one's occupational status, nor do they touch upon how one's race or ethnicity may affect the relationship between years of education and occupational status. The following bivariate analyses further explore the relationship between ethnicity and immigration status, occupational status, and educational attainment. Examining mean levels of occupational status and educational attainment by ethnicity and family immigration status will provide a clearer picture of the associations explored in the correlation matrices. Table 2.4 compares the ethnic differences in mean levels of occupation and educational attainment by examining one's occupational status by education. This table demonstrates the integral role of ethnicity and country of origin when comparing the occupational status of foreign-born and native-born in the United States. This table clearly shows that the relationship between educational attainment and occupational status may be fairly positive and direct for native-born adults, but varies greatly for the foreign-born of different ethnicities. Later in the chapter, multivariate analyses will help to answer the questions of what might be affecting these differences by ethnicity and whether years of education, time in the United States, or English ability serve as key determinants in predicting an immigrant's occupational success.

Table 2.4: Mean Differences in Occupational Status by Educational Attainment for Native and Immigrant Adults

	Mean years of schooling		Mean occupational status		Less than high school		High school		Some College		College		Graduate	
	Native	Foreign	Native	Foreign	Native	Foreign	Native	Foreign	Native	Foreign	Native	Foreign	Native	Foreign
White	13.419	13.196*	43.121	43.871*	36.230	36.610	37.823	38.621*	42.806	42.509	50.890	50.224	56.620	55.257
	(2.60)	(3.84)	(11.39)	(12.14)	(6.21)	(6.69)	(6.90)	(8.89)	(10.46)	(11.14)	(11.99)	(12.01)	(10.98)	(11.08)
Black	12.527	13.898*	39.578	47.039*	35.360	36.563*	36.159	37.947*	41.448	41.975	48.393	62.601*	56.354	48.354*
	(2.57)	(3.79)	(10.07)	(14.48)	(5.87)	(4.90)	(6.52)	(5.83)	(10.65)	(11.51)	(12.11)	(6.62)	(8.96)	(16.70)
Mexican	11.934	6.932*	40.000	35.037*	35.468	34.639*	37.439	36.691	39.113	35.064*	46.229	42.511*	58.659	45.445*
	(3.84)	(3.84)	(9.88)	(4.91)	(5.01)	(3.76)	(6.69)	(7.68)	(8.84)	(4.975)	(11.39)	(12.26)	(6.71)	(13.79)
P. Rican	12.886	9.102*	37.798	35.182*	34.845	31.972*	33.915	35.535*	39.203	40.199	53.145	51.926	59.956	58.612
	(1.77)	(3.74)	(7.08)	(8.83)	(3.73)	(4.03)	(6.84)	(5.26)	(5.05)	(8.610)	(10.13)	(12.45)	(7.69)	(11.30)
Cuban	15.574	10.458*	48.894	38.340*	36.767	35.341	37.742	38.130	36.524	39.726*	49.172	46.541	63.831	50.603*
	(2.41)	(4.29)	(13.91)	(8.89)	(8.97)	(5.09)	(5.69)	(8.18)	(3.57)	(8.701)	(10.23)	(13.00)	(3.42)	(13.06)
Chinese	16.646	12.871*	56.627	43.602*	39.356	34.971	36.360	36.899	43.464	41.462	50.248	48.668	63.431	54.719*
	(2.03)	(5.18)	(11.61)	(12.54)	(10.18)	(6.80)	(5.49)	(8.32)	(10.25)	(10.50)	(11.26)	(12.32)	(4.32)	(10.65)
Filipino	12.039	14.366*	41.510	43.373	36.595	34.394	38.314	34.833*	41.921	40.091	49.115	47.328	55.165	52.013
	(2.48)	(2.98)	(10.03)	(11.94)	(7.81)	(5.79)	(7.49)	(4.31)	(9.09)	(9.648)	(12.25)	(12.00)	(10.07)	(13.28)

(Continued on next page)

Table 2.4: (continued)

	Mean years of schooling		Mean occupational status		Less than high school		High school		Some College		College		Graduate	
	Native	Foreign	Native	Foreign	Native	Foreign	Native	Foreign	Native	Foreign	Native	Foreign	Native	Foreign
Japanese	15.682	14.202*	48.458	45.189*	36.548	39.895	38.071	35.782	41.290	41.494	51.487	50.577	54.435	53.309
	(2.36)	(3.14)	(10.33)	(12.09)	(7.88)	(12.45)	(8.01)	(7.47)	(9.04)	(9.95)	(11.07)	(10.98)	(4.23)	(10.92)
Korean	13.565	14.219	45.160	38.920*	34.100	35.039	42.414	35.302*	42.517	40.016	47.992	38.403*	61.746	52.340*
	(3.62)	(3.36)	(11.67)	(9.12)	(0.00)	(6.28)	(12.72)	(5.54)	(9.86)	(9.52)	(9.66)	(7.66)	(5.89)	(12.53)
S.E. Asian	12.888	12.465	40.875	39.229	34.100	34.976*	34.240	36.730	34.100	39.242	64.380	49.194	64.380	53.859
	(2.62)	(4.67)	(13.46)	(8.35)	(0.00)	(4.94)	(3.85)	(7.62)	(0.00)	(6.14)	(0.00)	(13.23)	(0.00)	(12.30)
S. Asian	14.125	15.252*	44.402	52.983*	36.106	37.137	36.010	38.902	42.973	43.822	48.566	46.268	55.913	60.920
	(3.00)	(3.66)	(11.41)	(13.23)	(7.64)	(7.89)	(1.77)	(9.35)	(10.73)	(11.85)	(9.79)	(12.05)	(11.61)	(7.99)
P.Islander	12.803	11.444*	41.808	38.247*	36.738	36.563	38.876	34.737*	41.425	42.775	55.493	44.472	58.376	53.520
	(2.29)	(3.42)	(10.83)	(8.92)	(6.51)	(8.09)	(8.37)	(2.94)	(9.96)	(11.44)	(11.23)	(11.84)	(8.83)	(0.00)
TOTAL	13.274	11.626*	42.585	41.714*	35.997	35.287*	37.614	40.614*	42.381	40.618*	50.678	50.595	56.805	53.886*
	(2.66)	(4.96)	(11.26)	(12.01)	(6.08)	(4.61)	(6.87)	(6.87)	(10.36)	(11.27)	(12.01)	(12.54)	(10.69)	(13.54)

Source: 5% Public Use Micro-Sample of the 1990 U.S. Census

Sample: all adults age 28-55; foreign-born adults arrived to the U.S. after age 23

Note: Standard deviations in parentheses

*p<.001 foreign different from native

In general, immigrants have fewer years of schooling and a lower occupational status than their native-born counterparts for most ethnic groups. This appears to be the case for Mexican, Puerto Rican, Cuban, Chinese, Japanese, and Pacific Islander immigrants. Immigrants from the Afro-Caribbean and Africa (denoted as "Black"), and from South Asia have the opposite relationship with their native-born counterparts. African-Americans and South Asians born in the United States have significantly fewer years of schooling and lower occupational status than their immigrant counterparts. The mean differences for these ethnic groups seem to uphold the straight-line depiction of status attainment for adults: years of schooling is directly positively associated with one's occupational status.

However, there are groups for whom this straight-line scenario does not fit:

- Immigrants from Northern or Western Europe, Australia or Israel ("White") have significantly fewer years of schooling than native-born counterparts who define themselves as being ethnically white, yet they have a significantly (albeit only slightly) higher occupational status than their native-born counterparts.
- Puerto Ricans born on the island with less than a high school education have significantly lower mean levels of occupational status than Puerto Ricans born on the mainland with less than a high school education. Yet, island-born Puerto Ricans with a high school degree tend to have significantly higher occupational status than mainland-born Puerto Ricans with the same years of schooling.
- Mexican, Cuban, Chinese, and Korean foreign adults with a graduate degree have lower mean occupational status than their native-born counterparts with the same schooling. It appears that for these groups, they get less occupational returns to their years of education than a native-born person of the same ethnicity and graduate education would. In general, foreign-born adults tend to have lower mean levels of occupational status than their native-born counterparts with the same years of education.
- Additionally, Filipino immigrants have significantly more years of schooling than their native-born counterparts, by over

two years, yet there does not seem to be an appreciable difference in occupational status between native and immigrant Filipinos.

• There does not seem to be much difference between years of schooling for Korean immigrants and natives, yet Korean immigrants have a significantly lower occupational status than their native ethnic counterparts.

In summary, Table 2.4 suggests that not every ethnic group's occupational success in the United States labor market is positively associated with its educational attainment; adults of different ethnic descent have somewhat different patterns of status attainment. Particularly for Filipino and Korean immigrants, greater educational attainment does not guarantee a higher occupational status. Being a Filipino or Korean immigrant seems to be a hindrance, rather than an invitation for opportunity.

One factor that could be contributing to the lack of social status relative to years of education for Korean or Filipino immigrant families is the language barrier to securing a job. However, Filipinos do have a grasp of English: all courses in private schools are taught in English and students in public schools are expected to be proficient in English. Other immigrant populations such as the Mexicans, Chinese or Japanese that do have a clear positive relationship between educational attainment and occupational status do not speak English as their first language.[5]

Why do these groups have a positive relationship between education and occupation, but the other groups do not? One reason for this difference may be the length of time the family or immigrant group has been settled in the United States. A longer period of settlement allows for greater enhancement of English language skills and greater assimilation into the opportunity structure and labor market of the United States. The multivariate analyses in the following section help to understand the interactions of immigration status with ethnicity, time in the United States, and educational attainment in order to disentangle the effect of being an immigrant from the effect of educational attainment and level of assimilation into the United States.

MULTIVARIATE ESTIMATES OF DIFFERENCES IN OCCUPATIONAL STATUS

The following analyses capture the relative effects of human capital and assimilation of the immigrant adult into the linguistic and social mainstream of the United States. I use ordinary least square regression to understand how the dependent variable (occupational status, measured as SEI) is affected by a number of independent variables that measure adults' social and economic characteristics. I estimate four separate models, which sequentially introduce the variables for educational attainment, mean level of education in country of origin (U.S. if native-born), whether the respondent arrived within the last five years, English ability, and age.

Table 2.5 provides a clear picture of the effects of ethnicity, educational attainment and assimilation factors by immigration status. In this table, foreign-born adults in the United States do not have as high an occupational status as natives (b=-0.225 in Model 1). However, once we control for education, this trend reverses and we see that foreigners with the same level of education as natives tend to have a higher occupational status (Model 2). This differential quickly fades once assimilation of the respondent is considered, yet one's educational attainment remains an important factor in predicting occupational status, even when controlling for race or ethnicity, English ability, whether the respondent is a new arrival in the U.S., or age.

Black, Puerto Rican, Filipino, Korean, and South East Asian adults have slightly lower occupational status than the reference group, white. This relationship holds even after we include educational attainment and assimilation factors. This suggests that for these sub-group populations their ethnicity remains a barrier to their achieving a given level of occupational status, when compared to the success possible for a white adult who has the same educational credentials, time in the United States (if foreign-born), English ability, and age. For other groups the opposite is true: even with the same educational attainment as their white counterparts, Cubans, Chinese, Japanese, and to a lesser extent, Mexicans and South Asians will have a higher occupational status.

Table 2.5: Ordinary Least Square Regression Analysis of Effects of Immigration Status and Educational Attainment on Occupation

Dependent variable = Socio-Economic Status Index of Occupation in 1990 (29.44-63.84)
Reference group = "White"

	Model 1	Model 2	Model 3	Model 4
R^2	0.024	0.276	0.277	0.282
Constant	43.28*	13.54*	23.30*	17.41*
	(0.020)	(0.092)	(0.564)	(0.606)
Foreign	-0.225±	3.241*	-1.390*	-1.659*
	(0.111)	(0.101)	(0.269)	(0.280)
Education		2.172*	2.169*	2.180*
		(0.006)	(0.006)	(0.007)
Mean country education			-0.797*	-0.816*
			(0.045)	(0.045)
Arrived within five years				2.386*
				(0.162)
English ability				0.614*
				(0.038)
Age				0.076*
				(0.001)
Black	-2.925*	-1.472*	-1.677*	-1.647*
	(0.056)	(0.049)	(0.049)	(0.049)
Mexican	-3.883*	0.311*	0.390*	1.167*
	(0.096)	(0.084)	(0.084)	(0.091)
Puerto Rican	-6.734*	-3.703*	-3.640*	-2.717*
	(0.100)	(0.081)	(0.081)	(0.090)
Cuban	2.255*	0.493	0.693*	1.777*
	(0.358)	(0.289)	(0.287)	(0.293)
Other Latino	-1.340*	1.134*	0.696*	0.911*
	(0.188)	(0.172)	(0.176)	(0.176)
Chinese	9.035*	3.901*	4.461*	4.763*
	(0.335)	(0.254)	(0.247)	(0.244)
Filipino	-0.084	-3.912*	-3.190*	-3.084*
	(0.357)	(0.340)	(0.339)	(0.341)
Japanese	3.892*	-0.089	0.574*	0.797±
	(0.325)	(0.287)	(0.282)	(0.282)

(continued on next page)

Table 2.5: (continued)

Dependent variable = Socio-Economic Status Index of Occupation in 1990 (29.44-63.84)
Reference group = "White"

	Model 1	Model 2	Model 3	Model 4
Korean	-3.448*	-8.091*	-5.498*	-5.049*
	(0.362)	(0.362)	(0.384)	(0.387)
South East Asian	-3.646*	-3.008*	-4.663*	-4.155*
	(0.371)	(0.403)	(0.416)	(0.425)
South Asian	9.285*	0.927*	-0.657	-1.336*
	(0.414)	(0.331)	(0.349)	(0.345)
Pacific Islander	-1.778±	-0.092	-0.252	-0.079
	(0.560)	(0.520)	(0.524)	(0.522)

N = 486,058

Source: 5% Public Use Micro-Sample of the 1990 U.S. Census

Sample: all adults age 28-55; all immigrants arrived after age 23

Notes: Person-level weight applied to account for sampling

              Huber/White standard errors in parentheses

[+]p<.05, ±p<.01, *p<.001

A key assumption underlying the models shown in Table 2.5 is that the effect of the different variables is identical for both foreign-born and native-born adults. In the next set of models, I relax the assumption by interacting the variable "foreign-born" with all the other variables. These interactive models allow me to test statistically whether, for example, educational attainment works differently for foreign-born or native-born individuals from the same ethnic group in terms of its effect on occupational status.

The interaction effects in Table 2.6 show that educational attainment is more important for native-born adults than foreign-born adults in predicting their occupational status. Across all the Models, each year of education will garner a native-born adult approximately 2.3 occupational status points, but each year of education garners a foreign-born adult with only about one occupational status point.

Table 2.6: Ordinary Least Square Regression Analysis of Effects of Education, Ethnicity, and Immigration Status on Occupation Status with Interactions

Dependent variable = Socio-Economic Status Index of Occupation in 1990 (29.44-63.84)
Reference = native-born "Whites"

	Model 1	Model 2	Model 3	Model 4
R^2	0.033	0.285	0.290	0.298
Constant	43.23*	11.49*	222.41*	221.08*
	(0.020)	(0.100)	(4.762)	(4.767)
Foreign	0.700±	16.649*	-201.78*	-207.18*
	(0.228)	(0.299)	(5.041)	(5.051)
Years of education		2.323*	2.325*	2.350*
		(0.007)	(0.007)	(0.007)
(Foreign * education)		-1.135*	-1.159*	-1.531*
		(0.018)	(0.018)	(0.020)
Mean country education			-17.220*	-17.549*
			(0.389)	(0.388)
(Foreign * mean education)			18.064*	18.166*
			(0.428)	(0.427)
Arrived within five years				1.510*
				(0.165)
(Foreign * recent arrival)				dropped[a]
English ability				0.376*
				(0.047)
(Foreign * English)				2.743*
				(0.082)
Age				0.080*
				(0.001)
(Foreign * age)				-0.060*
				(0.010)
Black	-3.450*	-1.438*	-1.438*	-1.381*
	(0.056)	(0.050)	(0.050)	(0.049)
(Foreign * Black)	5.711*	3.132*	7.905*	5.391*
	(0.337)	(0.298)	(1.107)	(1.092)

(continued on next page)

Table 2.6: (continued)

Dependent variable = Socio-Economic Status Index of Occupation in 1990 (29.44-63.84)
Reference = native-born "Whites"

	Model 1	Model 2	Model 3	Model 4
Mexican	-2.455*	-0.215*	-0.074	0.424*
	(0.111)	(0.093)	(0.093)	(0.099)
(Foreign * Mexican)	-6.211*	-1.597*	0.097	2.302*
	(0.267)	(0.257)	(0.481)	(0.477)
Puerto Rican	-6.300*	-4.071*	-3.889*	-3.094*
	(0.100)	(0.082)	(0.085)	(0.094)
(Foreign * Puerto Rican)	-3.262*	-0.100	1.509±	5.021*
	(0.389)	(0.321)	(0.506)	(0.513)
Cuban	6.061*	1.569*	1.551*	2.608*
	(0.445)	(0.332)	(0.319)	(0.319)
(Foreign * Cuban)	-11.82*	-4.362*	-2.701*	-0.748
	(0.646)	(0.560)	(0.656)	(0.669)
Other Latino	-1.687*	0.133	0.125	0.582
	(0.460)	(0.404)	(0.401)	(0.404)
(Foreign * Other Latino)	-0.527	0.523	3.329*	4.000*
	(0.540)	(0.478)	(0.761)	(0.762)
Chinese	16.430*	8.192*	8.681*	8.767*
	(0.304)	(0.226)	(0.234)	(0.231)
(Foreign * Chinese)	-16.64*	-8.175*	-7.572*	-4.998*
	(0.551)	(0.448)	(0.514)	(0.510)
Filipino	-1.491*	-0.477	-0.466	-0.069
	(0.627)	(0.621)	(0.622)	(0.626)
(Foreign * Filipino)	0.889	-1.48†	-0.112	0.126
	(0.783)	(0.755)	(0.811)	(0.816)
Japanese	4.399*	0.498	0.656‡	0.907±
	(0.348)	(0.295)	(0.298)	(0.298)
(Foreign * Japanese)	-3.414*	-1.004	-2.333±	-0.073
	(0.915)	(0.832)	(0.859)	(0.875)
Korean	2.726	2.262	2.216	2.666
	(2.068)	(1.826)	(1.829)	(1.845)
(Foreign * Korean)	-7.376*	-8.087*	-8.548*	-6.313±
	(2.109)	(1.866)	(1.872)	(1.892)

(continued on next page)

Table 2.6: (continued)

Dependent variable = Socio-Economic Status Index of Occupation in 1990 (29.44-63.84)
Reference = native-born "Whites"

	Model 1	Model 2	Model 3	Model 4
South East Asian	-4.799	-2.532	-2.120	-1.648
	(3.245)	(2.409)	(2.336	(2.368)
(Foreign * South East Asian)	0.247	-0.208	3.454	3.882
	(3.272)	(2.439)	(2.521)	(2.548)
South Asian	0.681	-0.922	-0.891	-0.477
	(1.709)	(1.355)	(1.345)	(1.326)
(Foreign * South Asian)	8.013*	6.374*	10.497*	8.680*
	(1.771)	(1.415)	(1.650)	(1.629)
Pacific Islander	-1.031	0.725	0.768	0.975
	(0.621)	(0.562)	(0.562)	(0.557)
(Foreign * Pacific Islander)	-5.356*	-4.671*	-1.515	-2.534
	(1.294)	(1.204)	(1.382)	(1.421)

N = 486,058

Source: 5% Public Use Micro-Sample of the 1990 U.S. Census
Sample: all adults age 28-55; all immigrants arrived after age 23
Notes: Person-level weights applied to account for sampling
           Huber/White standard errors in parentheses
[+]p<.05, ±p<.01, *p<.001
[a] dropped because of insufficient sample size

These findings run counter to the story detailed in the correlation matrices. The correlations between educational attainment and occupational status for immigrant and native-born adults were both about 0.4, yet the coefficients in Table 2.6 suggest that the relative effects of educational attainment on occupation are different for immigrant and native adults. Most likely this incongruity is due to the fact that immigrants are concentrated in the lower levels of educational attainment, where the returns to education are relatively low. And, as shown in Table 2.2, the standard deviations for mean educational attainment of immigrants are somewhat larger than those for natives. The greater variance in mean levels of education for immigrants may thus explain why the correlation matrices tell one story about the relationship between education and occupation for immigrants and natives, yet the regression analyses tell another.

English ability is also an important factor in occupational status for both native and foreign-born adults. As would be expected, English ability is a much stronger element for foreign adults than it is for native adults because most people born in the United States have a strong command of the English language. In fact, having a strong grasp of English can improve a foreign-born person's occupational status by as much as three points compared to a native-born person.

One striking example of the differences between native and foreign-born adults is that for Afro-Caribbean or African immigrants and their native African-American counterparts (termed Black in all tables). Table 2.6 shows that across the models, native-born blacks have lower occupation status scores than the reference group, white natives ($b=-3.45$ in Model 1). This relationship holds even after we consider the educational attainment of the respondent and other controls. Immigrant blacks, however, seem to find great success in the occupation market ($b=5.711$ in Model 1). And, their success over their native-born black peers in relation to the reference group of white natives remains consistent when we consider educational attainment and assimilation ($b=5.391$ in Model 4).

These findings suggest that even with the same years of schooling, black immigrants will have better success in the occupation labor market than native-born blacks. This finding lends support to Waters' (2001; see also Waters & Eschbach, 1995) research on West Indian immigrants. In participant observation and through a series of interviews in New York City, Waters found that West Indians had more occupational opportunities available to them than American-born blacks. Employers were more amenable to hiring immigrant blacks than native blacks because they perceived West Indians as being more agreeable on the job and more reliable.

Mexican immigrants follow a different trend than black immigrants: they have lower occupational status than their native-born counterparts, and do significantly less well in the occupational market place than whites ($b=-2.455$ for Mexicans and $b=-6.211$ for foreign Mexicans in Model 1). This holds true even when controlling for educational attainment in Model 2 ($b=-0.215$ for Mexicans and $b=-1.597$ for foreign Mexican). However, once we consider English ability and years in the United States as well as age, the Mexicans actually have slightly higher occupational status scores than their white counterparts (b=0.424 in Model 4) and foreign Mexicans have somewhat higher occupational status scores (b=2.302)—although these effects are fairly small. In general, then, both native-born and foreign Mexicans do not have as high occupational status as native whites, even if they each have the same years of education (as shown in Model 2). However, if the Mexican native or foreigner has the same English ability, has been in the United States for the same time, and is of the same age, their occupational status will actually be higher than their white counterpart (as shown in Model 4).

Chinese respondents also have striking differences between foreign-born and native respondents. When examined without any controls, Chinese immigrants do less well than native-born Chinese, but not any differently than native-born whites (b=16.430 for Chinese natives and b=-16.644 for foreign Chinese in Model 1). This relationship holds when we consider educational attainment: Chinese natives will still have a higher occupational status than native whites even if they have the same educational attainment, but foreign Chinese will not be any different (b=8.192 for native Chinese and -8.175 for foreign Chinese in Model 2). After considering time in the U.S., English ability, and age, Chinese immigrants will have a higher occupational status scores than whites (b=8.767 for native Chinese and -4.998 for foreign Chinese in Model 4). Through time, foreign-born Chinese will eventually do better than their white counterparts, but will still not do as well as native-born Chinese, even with the same English ability or educational attainment.

CONCLUSIONS

The mean differences in educational attainment and occupational status presented for foreign-born and native-born adults in the United States earlier in this chapter demonstrated that the status attainment process for immigrant adults does not seem to vary greatly by ethnic group: educational attainment remains a key component of occupational status even when controlling for country of origin, mean levels of education, the respondent's length of time in the United States and English ability. However, once we examined the interaction between immigration status and ethnicity in Table 2.6, a different story unfolds. Educational attainment remains a clear determinant for occupational status for both immigrant and native respondents, but the relative importance of education varied between foreigners and natives. Furthermore, the variety in occupational status for immigrant and native respondents of different races and ethnicities, even when controlling for educational attainment and assimilation into the social and economic mainstream of the United States (presented in Table 2.6), suggests that rather than a "straight-line" assimilation process, there are a variety of ways that educational attainment can produce a certain occupational status.

If immigration status, educational attainment, or even time in the United States and English ability explained differences in occupational status, one would expect the differences among ethnic groups to disappear once these factors were controlled. Likewise, differences remain between foreign-born and native-born adults even after the above variables are controlled. The fact that differences in occupational status do remain among ethnic groups and by immigration status suggests that something beyond educational attainment or assimilation is causing these differences. Chapter Three delves more deeply into the mediating variables that could be causing these differences by ethnicity to remain. In that chapter, I examine the effects of community context, social capital and ethnic capital on the relationship between immigration status, educational attainment, and assimilation with occupational status. Chapter Three also deepens our understanding of how these factors affect the educational attainment of these adults' offspring.

CHAPTER 3

The Effects of Community Context on the Occupational Status of Immigrant Families and on the Educational Attainment of Their Children

INTRODUCTION

Whether a community is stable with strong networks among its members or unstable and lacking in social and structural resources to assist the immigrant in securing a job could help or hinder immigrants translate an education into an occupation that uses those educational skills to their maximum. In turn, their child's schooling choices could be affected. This chapter examines how three important factors—social capital, societal reception or context, and ethnic capital—affect the occupational status of immigrant families and the educational attainment of children in those families.

Social Capital

Social capital—social resources within the network of ties available to the student in his or her community (Coleman, Hoffer & Kilgore, 1987)—is an important component of inter-generational transmission of status that can be embodied in a closely-knit ethnic community. As Coleman (1988) indicated, the greater social capital available to the family within a community should have positive effects on children's attainment even after parental social status is controlled. Some economic research does examine how networks and ethnicity affect entrepreneurship and labor market success of immigrant adults (see Borjas, 1990; 1993; 1994; Portes, 1995), but the connection to the child's potential status has yet to be determined. In fact, relatively little research on how social capital differentially affects the educational achievement or attainment of race, ethnic, and immigrant groups exists (Kao & Thompson, 2003).

Researchers who do look at the effect of neighborhood ties on schooling success often limit their analyses to assimilation patterns of second-generation children, rather than including immigrant children (Portes & Rumbaut, 1996; Portes & Zhou, 1993; Gibson, 1988). Even research that has included the term social capital, however, does not properly convey the neighborhood-level ties that James Coleman initially proposed, but rather uses within-school or within-family ties. For example, White & Kauffman (1997) define social capital as parental monitoring of student behavior and Stanton-Salazar and Dornbusch (1995) define it as teacher-student ties. Hao (1996) defines social capital as intra-family communication and relations. The central components of my definition of social capital are whether the student lives in or nearby an enclave with a high proportion of college graduates or people with a professional occupation, and the extent to which a student's parents are connected to that community via the network of friends of their child. This operationalization of social capital at the community-level allows us to determine how the density of friendship and acquaintanceship networks across families affects status attainment (Sampson, 1991) and takes into account the processes of social relations (Bankston & Zhou, 2002a).

Context

Recent research on children's educational attainment in immigrant communities attributes school success or failure to individual agency and socioeconomic status, together with "the social capital available to students, their cultural origin and history, and the socio-educational context that serves them" (Portes, 1999). Therefore, the socio-educational context in which the family finds itself is a factor in determining the occupational and earning potential of immigrant adults. In turn, researchers also claim that "context" is an important factor in the adaptation process of immigrant adults, and thus in the children's educational performance (Rumbaut, 1997; Zhou, 1992; Portes &

Rumbaut, 1996). This work on context, however, focuses on the reception, or "mode of incorporation" of the immigrant arrivals. Those immigrants who are "granted legal status, receive resettlement assistance, and are not subject to widespread discrimination... experience both faster economic progress and a smoother process of social and psychological integration" (Portes & McLeod, 1996). A favorable context of reception allows an immigrant community to build social networks and maintain its internal solidarity, and thus facilitates its members' accumulation of greater social capital. There is evidence that a favorable governmental and societal reception leads to faster socioeconomic mobility, a more positive self-image, and to better-integrated immigrant communities (Bailey & Waldinger, 1991; Light, 1984; Portes & Stepick, 1993; Zhou, 1992).

Ethnic Capital

Beyond the societal reception, other factors affect the occupational choices of immigrant adults and the schooling success of their children. One of these factors is "ethnic capital" (Borjas, 2000) in an immigrant community: immigrants potentially have denser networks in specific employment enclaves that native-born people may not have access to, which allows immigrants to succeed in one area of employment. Conversely, outside of those enclaves, immigrants may not have the same level of network and connections to allow them to find a stable, well-paying occupation. These networks may influence a child growing up in an immigrant family to drop out of school in order to get what he or she may consider a stable, good job.

Focus of this Analysis

Previous research that examines differences in educational attainment for children in immigrant families based on the context in which they live, rarely delves deeply into the composition of the immigrant family's community. By accounting for the immigrant adults' pre-arrival social status in addition to the family's post-arrival social status and the community in which the family lives, I am better able to measure the roots of a child's educational trajectory in the United States. Holding individual-level family socioeconomic status constant, I aim to find in what manner these community-level factors influence the child's educational attainment.

Analyses in this chapter shift the focus of analysis from the adult in the labor market to the family to fully map out the path of intergenerational status attainment. In order to test how social capital, societal reception, and ethnic capital affect the occupational status of an immigrant family and the educational attainment of a child in that family, I examine the percentage of immigrants and co-ethnics in the community, how many parents in a child's circle of friends the parents know, the residential stability of a community, and the percentage of upper-middle class residents in the community. I use data from the 1988-1994 waves of the National Education Longitudinal Study matched to contextual data from the STMP3 zip code files of the 1990 U.S. Census to ask first, whether available networks and density structures influence the post-arrival occupational status of a family; and second, whether those mediating variables, in turn, affect a child's educational attainment.

Studying the effects of a person's community on life-chances is not a new field of study (see Mayer & Jencks, 1989 and Sampson, et al., 2002 for thorough reviews of neighborhood effects on individual-level behavior among adolescents and recent work by Brooks-Gunn, et al., 1993; Foster & McLanahan, 1996; Ainsworth, 2002; Crowder & South, 2003 on neighborhood effects on educational attainment). Previous research often focuses on comparing blacks and whites (Duncan, 1994; Roscigno, 1999), but much research remains to be done about how immigrant youth are affected by neighborhood conditions, particularly whether children from racial and ethnic minority groups and immigrant families have access to more or less social capital than their native-born or white counterparts (Kao, 2004; Bankston and Zhou, 2002b). This work differs from previous approaches. I look specifically at different ethnic and immigrant groups and consider the pre-arrival social status of the parents, allowing me to disentangle the effects of social status and neighborhood economic and social attributes.

The analyses in this chapter show that social capital has a strong positive effect for native parents' securing a high occupational status, but does not have as strong an effect for immigrant parents: the social ties that are often said to explain employment opportunities operate more for native families than immigrant families. Furthermore, the density of ties within a family's social circle has a stronger effect on the educational attainment of a child in a native family than it does for a child in an immigrant family. I also find that the years of schooling of one's parents has the strongest impact on determining how far in school a child will go, beyond the social context in which the family lives. From these findings, I conclude that educational attainment of immigrant parents is not the only predictor that has an effect on the educational attainment of their children. In fact, the effect of immigrant parents' educational attainment disappears once we consider the community context of the family and the post-arrival occupational status, suggesting that post-arrival indicators also have an effect on a child's educational attainment. Evidently, the "American Dream" is still available for immigrant families: the educational attainment of parents does not necessarily predetermine the educational attainment of their children.

RESEARCH QUESTIONS

Two questions guide the research in this chapter. First, is the child's educational attainment closely aligned with the parents' educational attainment, as the traditional status attainment model would lead us to hypothesize, or will the family's post-arrival social status, measured as occupation and income, be more important in determining the relationship between the educational attainment of the parent and child?

I hypothesize that immigrant adults with a higher education, and thus potentially higher occupational status in country of origin, would be better able to translate their education into a high-status occupation once in the United States. This would result in a higher income, living in a neighborhood with a stronger school district, and potentially greater years of schooling for their children than for those adults who either had a low occupation in the country of origin, or for those adults who had a high occupation, but were not able to achieve the same kind of occupational prestige upon arrival in the United States. If after controlling for post-arrival occupational status, pre-arrival education still has an effect, then there is reason to believe that a person's education before coming to the United States will affect their child above and beyond the current social position the family finds itself.

Second, does the community that the immigrant family assimilates into affect the schooling success of their children: are the community contextual advantages or disadvantages that immigrant adults experience transmitted to their children?

The theory of segmented assimilation contends that immigrants are assimilating into different segments of the United States labor market and into different communities based on the mode of incorporation and context of reception from the U.S. government and the relative educational attainment of the parents. I hypothesize that if this theory holds, then the immigrants living in communities in which there are more economic opportunities and in which the immigrants are more established will have more occupational opportunities and their children will go further in school. Similarly, more developed economic resources within the ethnic community (ethnic capital) or stronger economic resources within the network of social ties of the families in the community (social capital) will also garner greater employment opportunities and the higher likelihood that the children in that family will pursue post-secondary education.

If I find that the effects of community social context, ethnic capital, or social capital remain after controlling for the human capital measures of the family before arriving to the United States, then my analyses will reinforce the theories of segmented assimilation, ethnic capital, and social capital. Therefore, social context, above and beyond the pre-arrival human capital of the parents affects not only the occupational status of parents, but also the schooling success of their children. Otherwise, it will be clear that the parents' educational attainment, more so than the post-arrival community context, predicts the life-chances of the immigrant family and the children in that family.

DATA

I use two data sources to answer the above questions. I measure the pre-arrival and post-arrival socioeconomic status of the child's family and child's individual-level characteristics with data from the 1988-1994 National Education Longitudinal Study. I merge these data with data on the community context with the school-level measures constructed from 1990 Census STMP3 zip code data.

It is difficult to separate the effects of immigrant status, language ability, or minority status from one another. Although previous research offers vast amounts of information about school, home, and individual factors that influence achievement, it is difficult to analyze specific sub-group differences within certain ethnic or racial groups. The fact that these populations are often lumped into pan-ethnic groups as "Asian" or "Latino," given the unique background factors of specific sub-groups, is often cited as a serious detriment to studies on ethnicity and racial differences in educational attainment (Kao & Thompson, 2003; Kim, 2002). Fortunately, the National Education Longitudinal Study (NELS) separates Asian and Latino students into sub-groups.

The National Education Longitudinal Study provides data that are invaluable to evaluating the roles of parental social status, community context, and family's assimilation on the educational attainment of Latino and Asian youth. NELS utilizes a two-stage probability sampling design that selected a nationally representative sample of 24,599 students from 1,057 randomly selected schools. NELS began with a cohort of eighth graders in 1988 and followed them at two-year intervals. I use data from the base year (1988) through the third follow-up (1994). The base year student sample encompassed in-school youth only and included 26,432 students, from whom 24,599 usable questionnaires and 23,701 completed eighth grade tests were received. Parent questionnaires were completed for 22,651 of the students. There are 1,555 foreign-born students (70 of whom were born in Puerto Rico) and 20,674 native-born students in the base year. A third follow-up survey during the 1993-94 academic year collects data from students, out-of-school youth, parents and teachers. 14,915 students remained in the survey through the third follow-up in 1994.

NELS particularly suits the needs of these analyses because it oversamples Latinos and Asians. As discussed in Chapter One, both groups include large numbers of foreign-born youth and children of immigrants. In addition to the basic national samples, NELS includes several augmentations to provide more detailed information about "rare" subgroups. The Office of Bilingual Education and Minority Languages Affairs (OBEMLA) provided funds to NCES for a supplementary sample of approximately 2,200 eighth graders who were potentially non-English language minority or had limited English proficiency. This involved oversampling students in the sampled schools who had Asian/Pacific Islander or Hispanic surnames.[3]

My final sample includes public-school students who have information from the base year (1988) questionnaire through the third follow-up (1994) questionnaire and who have zip code information. I match the individual-level student and parent data from NELS to contextual data from the 1990 U.S. Census based on the zip code of the student's school, retrieved from the Common Core of Data. My final sample is 10,547 students from 761 public schools that have zip code information linked to them.[1] My sample only includes students who attend public schools because a public school's zip code will most likely be geographically close to, if not the same as, the zip code in which the family lives.

Because the NELS sample design involved probability sampling, disproportionate sampling of certain strata (e.g., oversampling of Asian and Latino students), and clustering (e.g., students within a school), the resulting statistics are less precise than they would have been had they been based on data collected from a simple random sample of the same size. Because of this sampling design, observations in the same cluster are not independent.[2] I accommodate the sampling design of NELS by using pertinent weights to account for the probability of subpopulation selection in the sample in each of the three waves, and I use Huber-White (or, Sandwich) standard errors to account for the cluster sampling methods.[4]

With this national, longitudinal study, I can look at a large group of immigrants of different racial and ethnic backgrounds over time. Although NELS does not provide country of origin, it does separate Latinos into Mexican, Cuban, Puerto Rican and "other" (predominantly Central and South American descent). It also provides sub-categories for Asian and Pacific Islanders into Chinese, Filipino, Korean, Japanese, South East Asian, South Asian, Pacific Islander, West Asian, Middle Eastern and Other Asian. This sub-categorization helps me pinpoint any differences in student's schooling success by ethnic background and is used as a proxy for country of origin. I limit the bulk of my discussion to ethnic subgroups that can be traced to a single country with sample sizes above 100 respondents: Mexican, Puerto Rican, Cuban, Chinese, and Filipino groups.[5]

VARIABLES AND ANALYTIC MODELS

Dependent Variables

I report two sets of analyses in this chapter, using two different dependent variables.

(1) Occupational Status of Parents of 8th-Grade students (SEI).
I code this indicator with the same method I used for measuring occupational status using the 1990 PUMS data in the previous chapter. Because the analyses in this chapter use the family as the unit of analysis, rather than the individual adult as the previous chapter did, I take the higher of the mother's and father's occupational status to construct a single scale of the family's occupational status. For those parents who marked "homemaker" or "never worked," I used their spouse's occupational codes. In order to only account for families that have a measurable occupational status, I drop responses if the respondent marked "homemaker" or "never worked" and there is no spouse or if the spouse also marked "homemaker" or "never worked."[6] The range of occupational status scores is 29.44 for a family in which the highest occupation for the mother or father is a laborer to 64.38 for a family in which the highest occupation for the mother or father is a professional.

(2) Educational Attainment of 8th-Grade Students in 1994.
This is categorical variable that indicates what type of schooling, if any, an eighth grader in 1988 has by 1994. The four categories I use are:

0. Not a high school graduate
1. High school graduate, no post-secondary education
2. High school graduate, entered a two-year associates or vocational degree program
3. High school graduate, entered a four-year bachelor's degree program.

Because the NELS data set does not have information on whether the students graduate from their post-secondary education institution, I consider their educational attainment in categories that measure what type of post-secondary school students decide to enter or not enter.

Because the outcome categories are clearly in a ranked order, but the intervals among the categories is not uniform, I analyze the likelihood for a student to be in one of the categories of the dependent variable with ordered logistic regression.[7]

Independent Variables

The main predictors of a student's educational attainment in which I am interested are: family's immigration status; family's social status; community context; and assimilation of family into "mainstream" economic and social structures of the United States. In addition, I control for various demographic characteristics of students. Below I explain how I construct each indicator and my rationale for incorporating each into the models.

Family's Immigration Status
Of particular concern in these analyses is a family's immigration status. "Immigrant" families are families in which both parents are immigrants. "Combined" are families in which only one parent is foreign-born. "Native" are families with two native-born parents. My analysis centers upon the differences among these three family types.[8]

Unfortunately, most current research on the educational attainment of children in immigrant households presents "immigrant" and "combined" families together—defining them both as "immigrant families".[9] I choose to differentiate these two family types because the amount of resources available to these families may differ. For example, linguistic or economic resources available to children who have one native-born parent could be greater than those available to the children who have two immigrant parents because of the implied increased social and economic assimilation of the family with a native-born parent. In addition, the immigrant who marries a native may be more assimilated than an immigrant who does not. Conversely, if the family lives in a highly concentrated immigrant neighborhood, the social capital available to the child in the form of close ties among adults in the community may be greater for a child of two immigrant parents than for a child of mixed parentage. The social connections or occupational opportunities may not be as available to parents in a mixed marriage as they could be to parents in an immigrant family.

Family's Social Status
I use two variables to measure family social status: the number of years of education acquired by both mother and father (before arriving in the United States if the parent is foreign-born) and the occupational status of a student's father and mother (post-arrival if the parent is foreign-born). I use the parent's self-report or the report of a spouse to determine educational attainment and occupation. If this parent-level information is missing, I use the student's response. Family education is a continuous variable that uses the higher of mother's or father's education before arriving to the United States. I chose immigrant parents who came to the United States at age 23 or older to capture years of schooling before arriving to the United States with some accuracy.

Community Context
I operationalize segmented assimilation with community-level variables based on the zip code characteristics of the child's school. I match the student-level data from the 1988 NELS file with 1990 Census information to construct four variables that measure the type of social community in which the child attends school: 1) percent of zip code residents who are of the same race or ethnicity as the student—based on the subgroup categorization used by NELS; 2) percent of zip code residents who are foreign-born; 3) percent of foreign-born that arrived between 1987 and 1990; and 4) percent of zip code residents who have lived in the same residence for the last five years. With these variables, I am able to measure the social context in which a family sends their child to school, rather than simply use the student's race or ethnicity as a proxy for the social environment as does most research that tests segmented assimilation (for example, Kao & Tienda, 1995; Hao & Bornstead, 1998).

The first and second measures of segmented assimilation test whether going to school in an ethnically or immigrant homogenous community provides more opportunities for occupational networks for the adults that can then translate into better life chances for the students or if they constrain occupational and educational choices because of tighter social closure and a lack of opportunities to move out of a small network system. My third and fourth measures of segmented assimilation are the percent of recently arrived immigrants in the zip code and the percent of residents who have lived in the school's zip code for five years or more. These variables measure residential stability, or commitment to the community. Going to school in a zip code with a large number of people who have lived in the area for many years signifies that the community is not transient, and thus might positively impact the child's decision to continue school beyond high school because of social cohesion (Ainsworth, 2002).

If I find that these community-level indicators are positively associated with parents' occupational status or with the likelihood that their child will continue on to post-secondary schooling when considering parents' educational attainment and other social status variables, then there is reason to uphold the theory of segmented assimilation, which states that immigrants assimilate into various parts of the social and economic structure of the United States, into a "segmented" labor market that influences how well the immigrant sub-group succeeds economically.

To test the availability and effects of social capital on the children's educational attainment, I use a measure of how many parents of a child's friends the child's parents know when the child is in the eighth grade, a commonly used indicator of social networks and social closure (Coleman, 1990; Morgan & Sørensen, 1999; Ainsworth, 2002). I construct a dummy variable that measures whether the parents of the child know "many or some" of their child's friends' parents. The reference category is the parent knows "none" of their child's friends' parents.

I measure the community-level social capital with a standardized index of "upper-middle class" neighbors, which I define as: 1) the proportion of residents age 25 or more in the zip code who are college graduates and who are employed with a professional occupation, a variable that has been shown to have clear positive effects on student academic achievement (Ainsworth, 2002); and 2) the median household income of zip code residents. This index measures the availability of role models in the community, and important consideration in the neighborhood effects literature (e.g., Brooks-Gunn et al., 1993 and Morenoff & Tienda, 1997). Although zip code is not an ideal measure of "neighborhood", the limitations of the data necessitate the use of this measure. Previous research (Corcoran, et al., 1992; Ainsworth, 2002) has relied on the use of zip code to define a community with relatively robust results.

If I find that the more friends of one's child a parent knows, the greater probability of that child attending post-secondary schooling, then we can safely say that social capital, in the form of networks, connections, and the density of ties among families in the community, has a positive effect on child's schooling. Alternatively, I may find that social control due to tight bonds within the community could negatively effect a child's educational attainment, resulting in a negative coefficient for this variable. I expect that given the previous literature on ties within immigrant communities discussed above, greater social capital results in a higher-achieving child, net of parents' educational attainment.

I operationalize ethnic capital with the interaction of student's race or ethnicity with the index of "upper-middle class" neighbors. If there is a high level of human capital available in an ethnic community, as Borjas' theory of ethnic capital suggests, then we should find that these variables increase a student's probability of attaining a bachelor's degree, above and beyond that child's parents' educational credentials. Conversely, if I find that these variables do not influence a child's educational attainment significantly more than a child's parents' educational attainment, then there is reason to believe that the availability of role models of the same race or ethnicity in a community are not the relevant factors that determine a child's status attainment potential. Consequently, there would be reason to believe that a child is not going to be hampered by a low amount of community human capital.

Assimilation of Family

In addition to the measures of social status and the context in which the students attend school, I also consider to what extent the parents are assimilated into the American linguistic, social and cultural mainstream.

The first assimilation variable I include is a dummy variable that measures if one of the immigrant parents arrived in the United States within the last five years. I expect that the longer the immigrant family has been in the United States, the more accustomed its members will be to the school system and labor market of the United States, and thus the family will be better able to navigate the child through school and the parents will be better able to navigate through the employment sector. I also control for the age of the parent. The older parent will be more financially solvent and accustomed to the labor market than a younger parent.

Another possible assimilation mechanism that I consider is English ability or "language capital" (Borjas 1994), which can be a determinant of how well an immigrant adult does in the labor market and how well an immigrant student may do in school (Grenier, 1984; White, 1997; White & Kaufman, 1997). I construct a five-point scale of the parents' English ability based on a self-report of how well the responding parent speaks, understands, reads, and writes English (0: not very well to 5: fluent).

Student Characteristics
Throughout the analyses of student educational attainment, I control for important child characteristics often considered in education literature such as the grade the student started his or her schooling in the United States (kindergarten if the child is native-born), the gender of the child, whether the child is foreign-born, and whether the child is "limited English proficient." I mark a student as limited English proficient based on whether the child attended either an English as a Second Language class or a bilingual education class in eighth grade (the first year of the survey), or whether the student ranks him or herself as "poor" on writing, speaking, reading, or understanding English.

Appendix B lists the variables I use in this chapter with their means and standard deviations. I compare my final sample using 1994 NELS data with the original 1988 NELS sample to show that the mean values of the variables in question are not significantly different. Correlation matrices of the independent and dependent variables are available in Appendix C.

In what follows, I first examine how a child's educational attainment varies by ethnicity, family immigration status, and family background. The next sections examine the effects of community context on a family's occupational status and on a child's educational attainment using a multivariate approach. A final section provides a summary of the main findings of the chapter.

EXPLORATIONS OF ETHNICITY, FAMILY IMMIGRATION STATUS, AND FAMILY BACKGROUND

Tables 3.1 and 3.2 compare how race and ethnicity, family immigration status, and family background relate to the context in which the child attends school. Table 3.1 compares the means of the dependent and the main independent variables in this analysis by race and ethnicity. Table 3.2 compares the means for the main dependent variables by the family's immigration status and parents' educational attainment. Differences in racial and ethnic background, immigration status, and parents' years of education are apparent on just about all the contextual and family background variables.

Table 3.1 shows that black, Mexican, and Cuban students—tend to attend school among their co-ethnic peers.[9] These ethnic group students go to school in areas with a relatively high mean percentage of neighbors with the same ethnicity. For a Mexican person, the mean percentage of their co-ethnic peers in the school's zip code is 38.1 percent, for blacks, it is 36.9 percent, and for Cubans, 35.8 percent.

Certain ethnic groups are in predominantly immigrant communities. The total mean percent foreign-born in a zip code is 7.1 percent. All ethnic groups in my sample, except whites, go to school in areas that house a larger percentage of foreign-born than this overall percentage of 7.1 percent. Of Latino groups, Mexican, Puerto Rican and Cuban students, in particular, go to school in neighborhoods with a relatively high proportion of immigrants (19.2, 29.2, and 46 percent, respectively). Some Asian sub-groups have a moderate mean percentage of immigrants in their zip codes: 19.5 percent for Chinese, 17.6 percent for Filipinos, and 15.8 percent for South East Asians. Filipino, Chinese, Mexican, and South East Asian students attend school in communities that hold a relatively high percentage of recently arrived immigrants to the U.S.: 38.6 percent, 38.8 percent, 39.6 percent, and 42.5 percent, respectively, of the foreign-born in the zip code arrived in the three years before the 1990 Census.

Table 3.1: One-way Analysis of Variance of Mean Differences of Key Variables by Race and Ethnicity

	Total	White	Black	Mexico	Puerto Rican	Cuban	Other Latino	Chinese	Filipino	S. East Asian	Korean	South Asian	Japan	Pacific Islander
Education in 1994[1]	1.78	1.82	1.60	1.46	1.29	1.59	1.82	2.60	2.13	2.28	2.52	2.68	2.34	1.59
	(1.02)	(1.00)	(1.06)	(1.03)	(0.99)	(1.01)	(0.93)	(0.69)	(0.74)	(0.83)	(0.74)	(0.57)	(0.82)	(1.01)
Father's occupation	42.30	43.35	38.32	37.29	40.02	43.19	42.91	47.28	44.76	41.97	49.12	55.26	50.55	42.84
	(10.92)	(10.92)	(9.10)	(8.95)	(10.38)	(10.78)	(11.37)	(13.53)	(11.04)	(10.94)	(10.71)	(11.01)	(10.94)	(11.45)
Mother's occupation	41.61	42.50	40.03	37.09	37.71	38.85	40.97	43.56	44.41	37.33	46.94	52.52	45.87	39.11
	(11.51)	(11.56)	(11.14)	(9.69)	(9.23)	(10.05)	(11.95)	(12.79)	(12.25)	(9.69)	(12.14)	(10.89)	(11.25)	(9.47)
% Same ethnicity	69.55	90.84	36.94	38.16	7.03	35.87	10.44	4.71	6.01	1.79	1.38	0.15	4.74	5.33
	(35.51)	(11.25)	(28.77)	(28.77)	(8.84)	(29.28)	(16.56)	(6.21)	(9.48)	(2.5)	(1.98)	(4.19)	(15.44)	(14.69)
% Foreign residents	7.29	4.13	7.26	19.22	29.22	46.07	14.41	19.59	17.63	15.83	11.32	11.46	12.37	12.38
	(10.88)	(5.53)	(12.18)	(14.98)	(14.03)	(26.07)	(15.91)	(15.98)	(14.89)	(14.26)	(10.99)	(9.23)	(10.68)	(11.39)
% Recent Foreign	30.03	26.97	33.08	39.66	32.24	32.66	36.28	38.81	38.60	42.56	33.47	35.67	35.75	35.39
	(18.56)	(18.77)	(18.82)	(13.48)	(13.34)	(10.85)	(15.04)	(14.05)	(13.38)	(15.84)	(13.98)	(12.12)	(12.89)	(14.99)
% Same Residence	70.38	69.30	72.94	72.30	76.80	78.45	70.37	75.91	68.43	73.67	71.83	74.25	73.89	72.09
	(13.21)	(13.63)	(12.18)	(11.87)	(8.37)	(7.68)	(13.08)	(8.95)	(14.55)	(8.21)	(11.92)	(11.44)	(11.21)	(11.42)
Parents know child's friends' parents	0.35	0.39	0.31	0.25	0.21	0.26	0.29	0.16	0.19	0.13	0.16	0.34	0.20	0.24
	(0.43)	(0.44)	(0.39)	(0.36)	(0.36)	(0.41)	(0.39)	(0.35)	(0.38)	(0.31)	(0.36)	(0.47)	(0.39)	(0.38)

(continued on next page)

Table 3.1: (continued)

	Total	White	Black	Mexico	Puerto Rican	Cuban	Other Latino	Chinese	Filipino	S. East Asian	Korean	South Asian	Japan	Pacific Islander
Index of upper-middle class[2]	0.00	0.04	-0.28	-0.35	0.07	0.21	0.04	1.03	0.35	0.24	0.16	1.16	0.99	-0.13
	(0.93)	(0.91)	(0.83)	(0.78)	(0.93)	(0.75)	(0.95)	(1.13)	(1.00)	(0.94)	(0.36)	(1.07)	(1.12)	(0.60)
Parents' education	13.47	13.71	13.04	11.6	12.82	13.11	13.29	14.49	14.88	13.24	15.49	17.28	15.33	13.59
	(2.53)	(2.37)	(2.14)	(1.50)	(2.70)	(3.13)	(2.78)	(3.50)	(2.20)	(3.08)	(2.65)	(2.54)	(2.30)	(2.62)
Parents' English	4.58	4.93	4.90	3.10	3.32	2.69	3.78	2.63	3.64	2.27	3.50	3.73	4.15	4.07
	(0.99)	(0.34)	(0.39)	(1.50)	(1.31)	(1.52)	(1.37)	(1.44)	(0.81)	(1.35)	(1.36)	(0.76)	(0.96)	(1.31)
	N=10,547	N=6,958	N=1,233	N=978	N=101	N=48	N=245	N=148	N=145	N=117	N=98	N=54	N=42	N=42

Sources: Student and Parent Files of the National Education Longitudinal Study (1988-1994) and 1990 US Census STMP3 Zip Code Files

Notes: All means significantly different from "white" at 0.05 level

Weights to account for sampling probability applied

Standard deviations in parentheses

[1] Range is from 0 (did not graduate from high school) to 3 (entered bachelor's degree program)

[2] Standardized (mean: 0, standard deviation: 1)

Table 3.2: One-way Analysis of Variance of Mean Differences of Key Variables by Family Immigration Status and Parents' Years of Education

	Total	Parents' Immigrant Status			Parents' Education			
		Immigrant	Combined	Native	<H.S.	H.S. grad	College	Graduate
Education in 1994[1]	1.78	2.06	1.58	1.78	1.16	1.47	1.94	2.53
	(1.02)	(0.95)	(1.05)	(1.01)	(0.99)	(0.97)	(0.96)	(0.73)
Father's occupation	42.30	42.50	40.31	42.62	34.26	37.87	43.69	56.61
	(10.92)	(12.19)	(10.36)	(10.83)	(7.01)	(7.47)	(10.21)	(10.13)
Mother's occupation	41.61	40.12	39.03	42.22	33.32	37.72	43.30	53.66
	(11.51)	(11.66)	(10.81)	(11.54)	(6.37)	(8.12)	(11.44)	(12.30)
% Same race/ethnicity	69.55	23.32	52.48	77.74	57.87	73.33	71.11	68.35
	(35.51)	(31.08)	(38.74)	(29.88)	(35.53)	(33.36)	(35.11)	(38.40)
% Foreign residents	7.29	22.84	12.23	4.67	12.74	5.79	6.68	7.32
	(10.88)	(17.21)	(13.79)	(6.86)	(16.10)	(9.83)	(9.77)	(8.63)
% Recently arrived foreign	30.03	39.74	33.23	28.37	33.97[3]	27.84[3]	29.78[3]	32.00[3]
	(18.56)	(13.56)	(17.32)	(18.85)	(19.33)	(19.36)	(18.09)	(16.84)
% Same residence within five years	70.38	74.59	71.72	69.66	70.69[3]	69.93[3]	70.28[3]	71.34[3]
	(13.21)	(10.04)	(12.83)	(13.49)	(12.90)	(13.65)	(13.28)	(12.18)
Parents know child's friends' parents	0.35	0.21	0.24	0.38	0.25	0.33	0.37	0.41
	(0.43)	(0.37)	(0.37)	(0.43)	(0.34)	(0.41)	(0.44)	(0.46)

(continued on next page)

Table 3.2: (continued)

	Total	Parents' Immigrant Status			Parents' Education			
		Immigrant	Combined[3]	Native	<H.S.	H.S. grad	College	Graduate
Index of upper-middle class[2]	0.00[3]	0.031[3]	0.00[3]	-0.03	-0.41	-0.23	0.08	0.71
	(0.93)	(1.12)	(0.99)	(0.89)	(0.70)	(0.75)	(0.90)	(1.21)
Parents' education	13.47	13.02	13.12	13.58	9.37	12.0	14.17	18.61
	(2.53)	(3.65)	(2.66)	(2.33)	(9.26)	(0)	(1.17)	(0.92)
Parents' English ability	4.58	2.39	4.12	4.90	3.66	4.71	4.71	4.70
	(0.99)	(1.47)	(1.07)	(0.35)	(11.74)	(0.79)	(0.75)	(0.66)
	N=10,547	N=948	N=438	N=8,220	N=1,206	N=2,869	N=5,205	N=1,092

Sources: Student and Parent Files of the National Education Longitudinal Study (1988-1994) and 1990 US Census STMP3 Zip Code Files

Notes: All means significantly different from each other at 0.05 level except those marked with a [3]

Weights to account for sampling probability applied

Standard deviations in parentheses

[1] Range is from 0 (did not graduate from high school) to 3 (entered bachelor's degree program)

[2] Standardized (mean: 0, standard deviation: 1)

[3] Means are not significantly different from each other

Index of "upper-middle class" residents in a zip code also differs by race or ethnicity. Chinese, South Asians, and Japanese students, in particular, go to school in more economically advantaged areas than other ethnic groups do. Conversely, black, Pacific Islander and Mexican students have significantly less role models living in their zip codes than the other ethnic sub-groups do.

A complicated pattern emerges from these mean percentages. Mexican, Puerto Rican, and Cuban students attend schools in communities that have a high concentration of immigrants. Additionally, Mexican and Cuban students go to school among their co-ethnic peers to a greater degree than do Puerto Ricans or any other ethnicity. If the ties that bind a community are based on ethnicity, then Mexicans and Cuban students would be doing better in school and staying in school longer than an ethnic group that does not live in a tight ethnic community. Conversely, one would hypothesize that Puerto Rican and the students of various Asian ethnic groups would not go as far in school because the ethnic supports are not as tight in the zip codes in which they go to school. However, in this sample, Cuban and Asian students (except Pacific Islanders) have greater years of educational attainment than Mexican and Puerto Rican students.

We can shed some light on this dilemma by looking to the parents' years of education and the proportion of residents with a professional occupation or with a bachelor's degree and the median household income, measured as the index of "upper-class" residents. Mexican and Puerto Rican students have parents with relatively low years of education (11.6 years and 12.8 years, respectively) whereas Chinese, Korean, South Asian, and Japanese parents have the highest parental education level (14.4, 15.4, 17.2, and 15.3 years, respectively). The parents of Cuban students tend to have more years of schooling than the parents of Mexican students (13.1 years). Additionally, Cuban students attend school in zip codes that have a higher index of "upper-middle class" neighbors than Mexican students do. This is also apparent for Asian youth. Mexican students, however, attend school in neighborhoods that have less availability of role models than any other ethnic group.

The Latino students that are concentrated in areas with large numbers of their co-ethnics (Mexicans and Cubans) or immigrants (Puerto Ricans and Cubans) have different educational attainments, leading us to question whether social capital, as measured by tight ethnic or immigrant bonds, can help or hinder a student's advancement in school. More clear are the advantages of living in a community with a high proportion of upper-middle class residents. This is apparent when we compare the differences in the index of upper-middle class residents among the different Latino and Asian students. It is quite possible that the overall socioeconomic status of the community may help students succeed in school, more so than the availability of co-ethnic or fellow-foreign-born networks and ties.

Table 3.2 shows that native families are more likely than foreign families to send their children to schools with their own race or ethnicity (77.7 as compared to 23.3 percent) and foreign families send their children to schools in communities with a higher percentage of foreign-born than native families do (22.8 as compared to 4.6 percent). Unlike the differences for ethnic groups, the index of "upper-middle class" residents in a zip code does not differ based on family's immigration status. Immigrants are going to school in zip codes with similar levels of role models as native-born families. Thus, although they are in largely immigrant neighborhoods, they are not in neighborhoods that are necessarily more economically depressed than largely native-born neighborhoods. Additionally, the neighborhoods in which they go to school are relatively more ethnically heterogeneous than the neighborhoods of native-born families.

How is it possible that, as a whole, children in immigrant households have higher rates of school completion and more years of schooling than children in native households, yet they do not go to school in communities that are any more or less privileged than native-born students? Students from different ethnic, immigrant, and social status backgrounds evidently have a varied school experience. Whether this experience is solely dependent on the socioeconomic status of the community in which the student lives—rather than simply the density of the ethnic or immigrant ties within that community, as these mean differences and correlations lead us to believe—is determined in the multivariate analyses below.

THE EFFECT OF COMMUNITY CONTEXT ON FAMILY OCCUPATIONAL STATUS

Occupational status and educational attainment often determine what type of community a family is a part of. Yet, community context may have an effect on a parent's occupational status, particularly for immigrants whose choices of residence, or where to send their child to school, may be less dependent on social status, and more dependent on who they know from their country of origin. Table 3.3 tests the effects of community context on occupational status.

Table 3.2 demonstrated that immigrant parents are more likely than native parents to send their children to school in a zip code that has a higher proportion of foreign-born residents, suggesting that they choose to be close to their own foreign counterparts. Because the causal arrow can flow both ways between occupational status and community context, in this section I briefly discuss how community affects occupation. I concentrate on how community affects the child's educational attainment in the following section.

In these analyses, the student's family is the unit of analysis. By using the family's characteristics, rather than an individual adult, I can better measure the student's home-life context, as well as the community context. To test the relative effects of being in an immigrant or combined family versus a native family, I interact family immigration status with the other variables. Model 1 includes family immigration status, parents' educational attainment, and mean educational attainment in country of origin of parents (for combined and immigrant families). Model 2 adds parents' assimilation characteristics (English ability, whether family arrived in the U.S. within the last five years). Model 3 tests the relative effects of community context variables (segmented assimilation and social capital). Model 4 tests the effects of ethnic capital. All models control for child's race and ethnicity and parents' age. The complete models are available in Appendix D.

Table 3.3: Ordinary Least Square Regression Analysis of Effects of Community Context on Occupational Status of Families

Dependent variable = Family occupational status (29.44-63.84)
Reference group = white child with two native-born parents

	Model 1	Model 2	Model 3	Model 4
R^2	0.351	0.359	0.369	0.370
Constant	6.910	0.238	-4.953	-5.268
	(3.880)	(4.006)	(3.905)	(3.847)
Parents' Characteristics				
Both parents are foreign-born	11.128	19.019	31.027±	30.316±
	(8.463)	(9.816)	(11.378)	(11.403)
One parent is foreign-born	36.310	43.012	41.470	40.976
	(22.398)	(23.806)	(22.248)	(22.419)
Parents' educational attainment	2.138*	2.116*	1.997*	2.000*
	(0.045)	(0.044)	(0.048)	(0.048)
(Education * both parents	-0.802*	-1.074*	-0.984*	-0.975*
foreign-born)	(0.137)	(0.154)	(0.151)	(0.151)
(Education * one parent	-0.087	-0.247	-0.187	-0.192
foreign-born)	(0.185)	(0.215)	(0.217)	(0.212)
Country mean education	0.970±	1.059±	1.473*	1.553*
	(0.323)	(0.365)	(0.356)	(0.349)
(Country mean * both parents	0.089	-1.483	-2.901[1]	-2.837[1]
foreign-born)	(0.968)	(1.138)	(1.157)	(1.162)
(Country mean * one parent	-3.427	-4.373	-5.196[1]	-5.097[1]
foreign-born)	(2.440)	(2.404)	(2.164)	(2.190)
Family Assimilation				
Family arrived in country within		-7.492	-6.470	-6.936
last five years		(8.069)	(7.423)	(7.511)
(Recently arrived * both parents		6.964	5.566	6.057
foreign-born)		(8.226)	(7.605)	(7.689)
(Recently arrived * one parent		3.774	2.414	3.052
foreign-born)		(8.395)	(7.825)	(7.905)
Parents' English		0.061	0.059	-0.035
		(0.455)	(0.464)	(0.462)

(continued on next page)

Table 3.3: (continued)

	Model 1	Model 2	Model 3	Model 4
(Parent's English * both parents		2.127±	2.087±	2.095±
foreign-born)		(0.649)	(0.660)	(0.665)
(Parents' English * one parent		1.203	1.042	1.050
foreign-born)		(0.733)	(0.807)	(0.815)
Segmented Assimilation				
% Same Ethnicity			0.0004	-0.002
			(0.008)	(0.008)
(Same race * both parents			0.050	0.053
foreign-born)			(0.028)	(0.028)
(Same race * one parent			0.028	0.031
foreign-born)			(0.029)	(0.029)
% Foreign			0.056^{+}	0.058^{+}
			(0.025)	(0.024)
(Foreign * both parents			-0.021	-0.017
foreign-born)			(0.046)	(0.045)
(Foreign * one parent			-0.134^{+}	-0.136^{+}
foreign-born)			(0.062)	(0.060)
% Recent Foreigners			0.020	0.010
			(0.008)	(0.008)
(Recent foreigners * both parents			0.008	0.002
foreign-born)			(0.038)	(0.039)
(Recent foreigners * one parent			0.043	0.044
foreign-born)			(0.044)	(0.044)
% Same residence			0.012	0.010
			(0.014)	(0.013)
(Same residence * both parents			-0.040	-0.035
foreign-born)			(0.066)	(0.066)
(Same residence * one parent			0.104	0.102
foreign-born)			(0.057)	(0.057)
Urban			0.327	0.301
			(0.434)	(0.430)
(Urban * both parents			0.225	0.201
foreign-born)			(1.285)	(1.281)
(Urban * one parent			-0.853	-0.572
foreign-born)			(1.400)	(1.395)

(continued on next page)

Table 3.3: (continued)

	Model 1	Model 2	Model 3	Model 4
Rural			-0.387	-0.374
			(0.450)	(0.449)
(Rural * both parents			0.519	0.669
foreign-born)			(2.160)	(2.149)
(Rural * one parent foreign-born)			1.364	1.274
			(1.928)	(1.931)
Social Capital				
Parents know child's			1.290*	1.280*
friends' parents			(0.311)	(0.309)
(Parents know many * both			-1.569	-1.701
parents foreign-born)			(1.066)	(1.075)
(Parents know many * one			-0.718	-0.608
parent foreign-born)			(1.212)	(1.197)
Index of upper-middle class			0.668*	0.743*
			(0.179)	(0.205)
(Upper-middle class * both			0.719	0.351
parents foreign-born)			(0.610)	(0.653)
(Upper-middle class * one			0.029	-0.153
parent foreign-born)			(0.824)	(0.856)
Ethnic Capital				
Black* index of				-1.006[1]
upper-middle class				(0.494)
Mexican * index				0.413
of upper-middle class				(0.558)
Puerto Rican * index of				2.554[1]
upper-middle class				(1.106)
Cuban * index of				4.136[1]
upper-middle class				(1.743)
Other Latino* index of				1.202
upper-middle class				(0.841)
Chinese * index of				-0.846
upper-middle class				(1.268)
Filipino * index of				1.811
upper-middle class				(1.575)

(continued on next page)

Table 3.3: (continued)

	Model 1	Model 2	Model 3	Model 4
Korean * index of				-0.573
upper-middle class				(1.203)
Japanese * index of				0.243
upper-middle class				(1.249)
South East Asian * index of				-1.252
upper-middle class				(1.002)
South Asian * index of				-1.090
upper-middle class				(1.426)
Pacific Islander * index of				-3.289
upper-middle class				(3.213)

Sources: National Education Longitudinal Study (1988-1994), International Educational
Attainment Data (2000), and STMP3 Zip Code Files from the 1990 U.S. Census

Notes: Huber/white standard errors in parentheses

            Weights to account for sampling probability applied

⁺p<.05, ±p<.01, *p<.001

Most notable in these analyses is that the educational attainment of
parents has a significant effect on the family's post-arrival occupational
status for all three family "types". However, educational attainment for
immigrant families does not have as strong a role as it does for native
families. In addition, the effect of educational attainment for combined
families is not significantly different from that of native families. In
this manner, the occupational status process seems to operate in much
the same way for combined and native families. The relationship
between educational attainment and occupational status for each of
these families holds across the models. Knowing English well is also an
important factor in a family's occupational status, particularly for
immigrant families.

Among the variables that test the effects of segmented assimilation
on occupational status, percent foreign-born in a zip code appears to
have a positive effect on family's occupational status (b=0.058 in
Model 4), yet a negative effect for combined families (b=0.058-0.136=
-0.0.78 in Model 4). Thus, the greater the percentage of foreign-born in
a child's school's zip code, the lower the occupational status for
combined families.

For native families, social capital is the only context variable that retains its effect on a family's occupational status. Whether a parent knows the parents in the child's circle of friends, and the index of upper-middle class residents in the zip code of the school where the child attends, each have a positive effect on the family's occupational status. The social capital indicators, however, do not have any kind of effect for immigrant families or combined families; the effect of social capital on occupational status for immigrant and combined families is not significantly different from the effect for native families.

To recap, I find: 1) that parents' educational attainment has a positive effect on occupational status for native, combined and immigrant families, but that this effect is relatively stronger for native families; 2) similar to the findings in Chapter Two, more years of schooling may not lead directly to as large an increment in occupational status in immigrant as it does in native families; and 3) social capital, whether measured as who parents know, or an index of upper-middle class residents in the zip code where the child attends school, has a positive impact on the occupational status of the family as well.

I now consider how these same social context variables affect the schooling success of the children in these families.

The Effects of Community Context on Student Educational Attainment

Table 3.4 shows how each of the particular characteristics of the student's community affects how far a child will go in school. Model 1 explores the relative effects of a family's immigration status on a child's likelihood to move into a higher educational attainment category. Models 2 through 4 examine the effects of segmented assimilation, social capital and ethnic capital separately; Model 5 combines all three theoretical explanations for why context would affect how far a child goes in school.

Because ordered logistic regression analysis uses cut points to determine the probability of a child continuing from one category of educational attainment to the next, the coefficients are somewhat difficult to interpret. To alleviate this problem, I interpret the results with caution, using relative terms. [10]

Table 3.4: Ordered Logistic Regression Analysis of Effects of Community Context on Child's Educational Attainment

Dependent variable = Post-secondary education in 1994
Reference group = white child with two native-born parents

	Model 1	Model 2	Model 3	Model 4	Model 5
cut point 1	-1.615*	-1.311*	-0.743*	-1.802*	-0.224
	(0.058)	(0.090)	(0.075)	(0.060)	(0.341)
cut point 2	-0.456*	-0.160[+]	0.541*	-0.599*	1.121±
	(0.039)	(0.079)	(0.068)	(0.040)	(0.345)
cut point 3	0.885*	1.193*	1.999*	0.839*	2.670*
	(0.040)	(0.077)	(0.070)	(0.041)	(0.346)
Family immigration status					
Both parents are foreign-born	0.355*				0.537*
	(0.108)				(0.147)
One parent is foreign-born	0.023				0.153
	(0.152)				(0.134)
Segmented assimilation					
% Same ethnicity		0.004*			0.001
		(0.0009)			(0.002)
% Foreign		-0.002			0.001
		(0.003)			(0.005)
% Recent foreigners		0.0001			0.0008
		(0.001)			(0.001)
% Same residence		0.004			0.005
		(0.002)			(0.003)
Urban		-0.343±			0.102
		(0.105)			(0.101)
Rural		-0.319*			0.186
		(0.078)			(0.105)
Social capital					
Parents know child's			1.513*		1.505*
friends' parents			(0.069)		(0.067)
Index of upper-middle class			0.474*	0.466*	0.481*
			(0.048)	(0.057)	(0.066)

(continued on next page)

84

Table 3.4: (continued)

	Model 1	Model 2	Model 3	Model 4	Model 5
Ethnic capital					
Black * index of				-0.319	-0.248
upper-middle class				(0.187)	(0.189)
Mexican * index of				-0.122	-0.066
upper-middle class				(0.125)	(0.139)
P.R. * index of				0.591	0.692[+]
upper-middle class				(0.302)	(0.297)
Cuban * index of				0.032	0.271
upper-middle class				(0.298)	(0.328)
Chinese * index of				-0.395	-0.328
upper-middle class				(0.246)	(0.281)
Filipino * index of				-0.234	-0.255
upper-middle class				(0.172)	(0.150)

Sources: National Education Longitudinal Study (1988-1994), International Educational Attainment Data (2000), and STMP3 Zip Code Files from the 1990 U.S. Census

Notes: Huber/white standard errors in parentheses

Weights to account for sampling probability applied

$^{+}p<.05, \pm p<.01, *p<.001$

Overall, a child with two parents who are foreign-born has a greater likelihood to go on to post-secondary education than a child of two native-born parents. Percent of residents in a zip code who are of the same race or ethnicity of the student, living in an urban or rural environment, the availability of role models in the zip code, and whether the child's parents know the parents in the child's circle of friends, are all significant predictors of how far in school a student will go. In Model 5, where all community-level variables are modeled together, it is apparent that the more social ties a parent has among their child's friendship network and the greater the proportion of upper-middle class residents, the farther in school a child is likely to go.

In the next table, I examine how the community context and family background operate to predict how far a child will go in school for children growing up in immigrant, combined, and native households. In each model, I control for the child's race or ethnicity, whether the child is a recent arrival to the U.S., grade the child started school in the U.S., and gender. The complete models for Table 3.5 are available in Appendix E.

Effect of Family Type

After controlling for family background, community context, and child's characteristics, children in immigrant families are more likely than children in native families to continue their post-secondary schooling. Children in combined families are not more or less likely than their native-born counterparts to go on to post-secondary education. Normally, we would hypothesize that combined families are more "assimilated" into the mainstream culture and thus would know how to navigate the system better than their immigrant counterparts. Instead, this finding suggests that combined families are more similar to native families, and that the children in both of these families have a lower probability of going on to post-secondary school than their immigrant counterparts.

This finding runs counter to the straight-line assimilation hypothesis that the more assimilated a student's family is to the prevailing mainstream culture and norms, the farther that student will go in school because of the greater knowledge of how to navigate the schooling and labor market system. These results show that rather than group families with one foreign parent and two foreign parents together, researchers need to group combined and native families together.

Because of the potential for immigrant adults to rely on within-family communication, we might expect to find that the higher the parents' educational attainment for native households, the farther in school the child will go. Years of schooling of immigrant parents, however, do not have the same predictive value for a child's educational attainment as it does in native families, net of all other variables.

Table 3.5: Ordered Logistic Regression Analysis of Effects of Community Context and Immigration Status on Child's Educational Attainment

Dependent Variable = Post-secondary education in 1994
Reference group = white child with two native-born parents

	Model 1	Model 2	Model 3	Model 4
cut point 1	3.387±	4.972*	5.804*	5.835*
	(1.041)	(1.157)	(1.241)	(1.268)
cut point 2	4.719*	6.396*	7.286*	7.320*
	(1.045)	(1.156)	(1.241)	(1.270)
cut point 3	6.321*	8.106*	9.034*	9.072*
	(1.048)	(1.156)	(1.242)	(1.270)
Parents' Characteristics				
Both parents are foreign-born	3.612	6.976±	6.788±	6.586[1]
	(2.162)	(2.355)	(2.531)	(2.576)
One parent is foreign-born	-2.630	-2.550	-0.398	-4.076
	(2.401)	(2.881)	(3.546)	(3.489)
Parents' educational attainment	0.242*	0.213*	0.165*	0.166*
	(0.015)	(0.015)	(0.016)	(0.015)
(Education * both parents	-0.165*	-0.146*	-0.144*	-0.154*
foreign-born)	(0.028)	(0.030)	(0.036)	(0.036)
(Education * one parent	-0.012	-0.022	-0.021	-0.015
foreign-born)	(0.046)	(0.050)	(0.053)	(0.051)
Country mean years of education	0.066	0.093	0.098	0.113
	(0.085)	(0.096)	(0.105)	(0.106)
(Country mean * both parents	-0.035	-0.0212	-0.085	-0.058
foreign-born)	(0.235)	(0.269)	(0.283)	(0.293)
(Country mean * one parent	0.430	0.468	0.894[1]	0.906[1]
foreign-born)	(0.273)	(0.305)	(0.377)	(0.370)
Family Assimilation				
Parents' English			-0.069	-0.089
			(0.104)	(0.105)
(Parents' English * both parents			0.261	0.265[1]
foreign-born)			(0.135)	(0.134)

(continued on next page)

Table 3.5: (continued)

	Model 1	Model 2	Model 3	Model 4
(Parents' English * one parent foreign-born)			-0.255 (0.003)	-0.258 (0.212)
Arrived within last five years			-1.842+ (0.866)	-1.831+ (0.924)
(Parent recently arrived * both parents foreign-born)			2.034+ (0.999)	2.052+ (1.039)
(Parent recently arrived * one parent foreign-born)			1.154 (0.985)	1.125 (1.027)
Parents' age			0.017± (0.006)	0.017± (0.006)
(Parents' age * both parents foreign-born)			-0.006 (0.016)	-0.008 (0.015)
(Parents' age * one parent foreign-born)			-0.032 (0.021)	-0.035 (0.020)
Segmented Assimilation				
% Same Ethnicity		0.001 (0.002)	0.001 (0.0020	0.001 (0.002)
(Same race * both parents foreign-born)		-0.008 (0.004)	-0.010 (0.006)	-0.009 (0.006)
(Same race * one parent foreign-born)		0.003 (0.006)	-0.000 (0.005)	0.000 (0.005)
% Foreign		0.006 (0.005)	0.005 (0.006)	0.005 (0.006)
(Foreign * both parents foreign-born)		0.002 (0.009)	0.003 (0.010)	0.001 (0.010)
(Foreign * one parent foreign-born)		-0.019 (0.014)	-0.018 (0.013)	-0.019 (0.013)
% Recent foreigners		0.000 (0.001)	0.000 (0.001)	-0.000 (0.001)
(Recent foreigners * both parents foreign-born)		-0.026+ (0.008)	-0.025± (0.009)	-0.024+ (0.009)
(Recent foreigners * one parent foreign-born)		0.001 (0.010)	-0.002 (0.010)	-0.001 (0.009)

(continued on next page)

Table 3.5: (continued)

	Model 1	Model 2	Model 3	Model 4
% Same residence		0.009±	0.008±	0.008±
		(0.003)	(0.003)	(0.003)
(Same residence * both parents		-0.019	-0.017	-0.016
foreign-born)		(0.001)	(0.012)	(0.012)
(Same residence * one parent		-0.00	-0.003	-0.003
foreign-born)		(0.012)	(0.012)	(0.012)
Urban		0.068	0.069	0.065
		(0.115)	(0.116)	(0.117)
(Urban * both parents		-0.266	-0.267	-0.242
foreign-born)		(0.221)	(0.231)	(0.232)
(Urban * one parent foreign-born)		-0.108	-0.048	0.014
		(0.345)	(0.306)	(0.302)
Rural		0.229±	0.306±	0.310±
		(0.105)	(0.104)	(0.105)
(Rural * both parents foreign-born)		-0.659	-0.752	-0.711
		(0.399)	(0.411)	(0.421)
(Rural * one parent foreign-born)		0.504	0.489	0.467
		(0.419)	(0.430)	(0.433)
Social Capital				
Parents know many or some of		1.426*	1.423*	1.425*
Child's friends' parents		(0.079)	(0.078)	(0.077)
(Parents know many * both parents		-0.897*	-0.941*	-0.910*
foreign-born)		(0.202)	(0.202)	(0.206)
(parents know many * one parent		-0.807*	-0.739±	-0.721±
foreign-born)		(0.261)	(0.252)	(0.248)
Index of upper-middle class		0.275*	0.244*	0.263*
		(0.057)	(0.056)	(0.059)
(Upper-middle class * both parents		-0.091	-0.941*	-0.214
foreign-born)		(0.112)	(0.202)	(0.131)
(Upper-middle class * one parent		0.098	0.154	0.116
foreign-born)		(0.135)	(0.124)	(0.123)

(continued on next page)

89

Table 3.5: (continued)

	Model 1	Model 2	Model 3	Model 4
Ethnic Capital				
Black* index of				-0.236
upper-middle class				(0.243)
Mexican * index of				0.066
upper-middle class				(0.147)
Puerto Rican * index of				0.880[+]
upper-middle class				(0.348)
Cuban * index of				0.375
upper-middle class				(0.233)
Other Latino* index of				-0.319[+]
upper-middle class				(0.155)
Chinese * index of				-0.287
upper-middle class				(0.298)
Filipino * index of				0.000
upper-middle class				(0.175)
Korean * index of				0.349
upper-middle class				(0.373)
Japanese * index of				0.134
upper-middle class				(0.326)
South East Asian * index of				0.767±
upper-middle class				(0.274)
South Asian * index of				0.205
upper-middle class				(0.390)
Pacific Islander * index of				1.316[+]
upper-middle class residents				(0.621)

Sources: National Education Longitudinal Study (1988-1994), International Educational Attainment Data (2000), and STMP3 Zip Code Files from the 1990 U.S. Census

Notes: Huber/white standard errors in parentheses.

Weights to account for sampling probability applied.

All models control for child's time in the U.S., grade when child stated schooling in the U.S., whether the child is LEP, foreign or female.

Models 3 and 4 control for parents' age, whether a parent arrived less than 5 years ago (for immigrant and combined families), and parents' occupational status.

[+]p<.05, ±p<.01, *p<.001

As an example of how the model can be interpreted to show the effects of the different variables, I calculate the predicted probabilities that a child in an immigrant, combined, or native family will enter post-secondary education for parents who have less than a high school education, holding all other variables at their means.[11] All other variables are set equal to their means so the only differences among families is the immigration status of families. Figure 3.1 graphs these predicted probabilities and shows that holding all variables at their mean, children in immigrant households whose parents have less than a high school education are much *more* likely to go on to some kind of post-secondary schooling than their counterparts who have one or two native-born parents.

Figure 3.1: Predicted Probabilities of Students from Different Types of Families Completing High School and Entering Post-secondary Education When Parents Have Less Than a High School Education

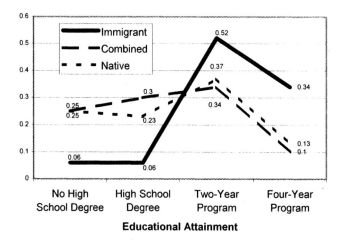

Effect of Ethnicity

In addition to differences among the three family types, ethnic differences in educational attainment remains. Table 3.6 is an excerpt from Table 3.5; it shows the coefficients for children of different race/ethnicities.

In Table 3.6, much of the ethnic group differences is explained in Model 4, which includes the interaction of ethnicity with socio-economic status of the community (ethnic capital), and the connections among parents and the parents of their child's friends (social capital), family background, and assimilation of the family. However, differences do remain. Across the models, students of Mexican, Puerto Rican, Cuban, and Filipino descent in immigrant families have a lower likelihood to enter a higher category of education than white students in immigrant families. These differences remain even when considering family background, social context, and child's characteristics. Chinese students are more likely than their white counterparts in immigrant families to go on to post-secondary education, all things being equal.

For children of native parents, Puerto Rican students have a lower likelihood to enter post-secondary schooling than their white counterparts. From these comparisons, we see that one ethnic group of students—Puerto Rican—continues to have lower educational attainment than white students. All else being equal, Puerto Rican children in immigrant and native households do not go as far in school as their white counterparts. Children who have one island parent and one mainland parent are not significantly more or less likely than their native-born counterparts to go further in school than white children.

Table 3.6: Ordered Logistic Regression Analysis of Effects of Community Context and Immigration Status on Educational Attainment for Children of Different Race/Ethnicities

Dependent Variable = Post-secondary education in 1994
Reference group = white child with two native-born parents

	Model 1	Model 2	Model 3	Model 4
cut point 1	3.387±	4.972*	5.804*	5.835*
	(1.041)	(1.157)	(1.241)	(1.268)
cut point 2	4.719*	6.396*	7.286*	7.320*
	(1.045)	(1.156)	(1.241)	(1.270)
cut point 3	6.321*	8.106*	9.034*	9.072*
	(1.048)	(1.156)	(1.242)	(1.270)
Black	-0.338^	-0.036	0.045	-0.041
	(0.133)	(0.210)	(0.216)	(0.286)
(Black * both parents	0.491	0.394	-0.201	0.109
foreign-born)	(1.313)	(1.275)	(1.306)	(1.336)
(Black * one parent foreign-born)	2.253	3.013	5.380'	5.647'
	(1.559)	(1.880)	(2.278)	(2.244)
Mexican	-0.218	0.020	0.031	0.016
	(0.168)	(0.207)	(0.228)	(0.245)
(Mexican * both parents	-0.769	-0.877	-0.813	-0.762
foreign-born)	(0.556)	(0.521)	(0.523)	(0.529)
(Mexican * one parent	1.113	1.697'	2.408'	2.479±
foreign-born)	(0.746)	(0.826)	(0.967)	(0.955)
Puerto Rican	-0.769	-0.599	-0.539	-0.617
	(0.472)	(0.581)	(0.552)	(0.489)
(Puerto Rican * both parents	-0.809	-1.439	-1.621	-1.581'
foreign-born)	(0.799)	(0.879)	(0.846)	(0.789)
(Puerto Rican * one parent	0.604	1.405	1.643	1.787
foreign-born)	(0.812)	(1.099)	(1.083)	(1.071)
Cuban	-0.159	0.018	0.201	0.253
	(0.276)	(0.347)	(0.351)	(0.399)
(Cuban * both parents	-0.817	-1.338'	-1.439'	-1.495'
foreign-born)	(0.582)	(0.649)	(0.684)	(0.731)

(continued on next page)

Table 3.6: (continued)

	Model 1	Model 2	Model 3	Model 4
(Cuban * one parent foreign-born)	0.029	0.611	0.691	0.386
	(0.854)	(1.127)	(1.168)	(1.212)
Other Latino	-0.304	-0.047	-0.086	-0.188
	(0.196)	(0.282)	(0.289)	(0.311)
(Other Latino * both parents	0.489	0.232	0.166	0.443
foreign-born)	(0.798)	(0.768)	(0.803)	(0.789)
(Other Latino * one parent	2.340[+]	2.728[+]	4.093±	4.527±
foreign-born)	(0.649)	(1.210)	(1.368)	(1.347)
Chinese	0.657	0.921	0.961	1.151
	(0.649)	(0.777)	(0.781)	(0.733)
(Chinese * both parents	1.261	0.757	0.555	0.671
foreign-born)	(0.938)	(1.088)	(1.041)	(1.009)
(Chinese * one parent	1.384	1.621	1.342	1.558
foreign-born)	(1.179)	(1.343)	(1.222)	(1.205)
Filipino	0.618	0.780	0.870	0.829
	(0.365)	(0.477)	(0.491)	(0.511)
(Filipino * both parents	0.618	-1.285[+]	-1.671[+]	-1.542[+]
foreign-born)	(0.365)	(0.653)	(0.688)	(0.698)
(Filipino * one parent	0.194	0.813	1.111	1.165
foreign-born)	(0.633)	(0.927)	(0.941)	(0.940)
Korean	0.975	1.429	1.396	1.222
	(0.760)	(0.891)	(0.903)	(0.891)
(Korean * both parents	-0.167	-1.308	-1.291	-1.430
foreign-born)	(0.921)	(1.232)	(1.263)	(1.259)
(Korean * one parent foreign-born)	-0.758	-0.675	-1.535	-1.413
	(0.990)	(1.244)	(1.246)	(1.237)
Japanese	0.375	0.286	0.179	-0.024
	(0.375)	(0.455)	(0.470)	(0.590)
(Japanese * both parents	-0.855	-1.638	-1.567	-1.501
foreign-born)	(0.697)	(1.090)	(1.138)	(1.165)
(Japanese * one parent	-1.262	-0.595	-0.879	-0.775
foreign-born)	(0.927)	(1.007)	(0.935)	(1.009)

(continued on next page)

Table 3.6: (continued)

	Model 1	Model 2	Model 3	Model 4
South East Asian	0.893	0.640	0.719	0.383
	(0.934)	(0.875)	(1.050)	(0.650)
(South East Asian * both parents	-0.146	0.137	-0.225	0.412
foreign-born)	(1.551)	(1.453)	(1.593)	(1.400)
(South East Asian * one parent	0.979	2.234	4.272	4.317
foreign-born)	(2.055)	(2.205)	(2.606)	(2.460)
South Asian	-0.141	0.623	0.738	0.748
	(0.864)	(1.052)	(0.916)	(0.908)
(South Asian * both parents	1.474	0.300	-0.345	-0.347
foreign-born)	(1.422)	(1.503)	(1.435)	(1.514)
(South Asian * one parent	dropped[a]	dropped[a]	dropped[a]	dropped[a]
foreign-born)				
Pacific Islander	-0.649	-0.086	-0.116	0.278
	(0.354)	(0.383)	(0.426)	(0.413)
(Pacific Islander * both parents	-0.144	-0.877	-1.358	-1.955
foreign-born)	(0.987)	(0.961)	(1.029)	(1.039)
(Pacific Islander * one parent	3.267	3.803	4.919[+]	5.311[+]
foreign-born)	(1.941)	(2.343)	(2.345)	(2.243)

Sources: National Education Longitudinal Study (1988-1994), International Educational Attainment Data (2000), and STMP3 Zip Code Files from the 1990 U.S. Census

Notes: Huber/white standard errors in parentheses.

        Weights to account for sampling probability applied.

        All models control for child's time in the U.S., grade when child stated schooling in the U.S., whether the child is LEP, foreign or female.

        Models 3 and 4 control for parents' age, whether a parent arrived less than 5 years ago (for immigrant and combined families), and parents' occupational status.

[+]$p<.05$, [±]$p<.01$, [*]$p<.001$

[a] dropped because of insufficient sample size

Three possible characteristics of Puerto Rican students may cause them to still do less well in school than their white counterparts in immigrant and native households. One possible factor is that Puerto Rican students straddle the two worlds of the mainland (the United States) and the island (Puerto Rico). The commonwealth status of

Puerto Rico contributes to great amounts of migration to and from the island. Return migration to Puerto Rico has been a significant component of the demographic picture of the island since the 1950s (Rivera-Batiz & Santiago, 1998). Circular migration is a phenomenon not peculiar to Puerto Ricans, but certainly dominates the cultural landscape. Census data show that as many as 130,000 circular migrants moved back and forth between the United States and Puerto Rico in the 1980s (Rivera-Batiz & Santiago, 1998). This constant movement of the families may have deleterious effects on the children. Unfortunately, the data I use does not ask students or parents about the family's circular migration patterns, so I cannot test this theory.

Second, Puerto Ricans are officially citizens of the United States, yet the island of Puerto Rico, the "country-of-origin," is a commonwealth of the U.S. and therefore not a state with full representation in Congress. This imprecise political state of Puerto Ricans in regards to the United States may be why Puerto Ricans often feel more culturally aligned with Latin America than with the United States (Morris, 1995).

Third, the cultural divide between mainland Puerto Ricans (those in the United States) from both mainstream American culture and the island culture may contribute to the lack of educational attainment for Puerto Rican children. The difficulty to form a coherent identity around a country may shroud the students' abilities to use ethnic capital or social capital in their communities to their benefit.

Effect of Social Capital

Table 3.5 also shows that social capital has a positive effect on a child's schooling. Knowing the parents in your child's circle of friends has a positive effect on a child's educational attainment for native families, and appears to have an effect for immigrant and combined families as well. The more social ties a parent has with the parents of his or her child's network of friends, the greater the likelihood that the child will move higher through school. We see clear differences based on immigration status of the family: this relationship is weaker for immigrant and combined families than it is for native families. For combined and native families, the greater the proportion of middle-class residents in the student's school's zip code, the greater the likelihood that a child will enter post-secondary school.

Table 3.3 showed that native-household parents have a significantly higher mean level of knowing the parents of their child's friends than immigrant-household parents. The social capital hypothesis would lead us to believe that these ties enhance the parents' capacities to watch over their children's schooling. In Table 3.5, knowing your child's friends does affect how far a child will go in school for each family type, yet the effect is strongest for native families. Children in native households whose parents have closer social ties with other parents in their child's circle of friends are more likely to go farther in school than children with parents who do not have these connections. However, all else being equal, an immigrant or combined parent's knowing his or her child's friends' parents does not have as much of an effect on the child's schooling decisions as it does for a child of native parents.

Social capital may not be as large a factor in the educational attainment of children in immigrant households as for children in native households, for a number of reasons. First, the community into which immigrant parents are making these ties consists of other foreign-born people. Table 3.2 showed that immigrant households send their children to school in communities where the mean percentage of foreign-born residents is 22.8 percent, and one-third of those foreign-born arrived within the three years prior to the 1990 Census, whereas native-born households live in zip codes with about 5 percent foreign-born. The concentration of immigrant householders into communities in which most people are newcomers may not offer immigrants the same opportunity structure of employment or information networks that native householders may enjoy. Thus, the ties that bind immigrant parents together in a student's community may not factor as much into that child's schooling success because the ties do not hold as much "capital." Second, the friends of students may not be of the same ethnicity or immigration status as their parents. Parents would then be reluctant and uncomfortable to reach out to the parents of their child's circle of friends. Because of these two reasons, parents may be more reliant on the family itself to help construct the learning environment for their children. Family support may be acting as a counterweight to the loss of community bonds.

Stanton-Salazar & Dornbush (1995) and Valenzuela & Dornbush (1994) suggest that immigrant families compensate for the absence of social capital in the form of outside networks by emphasizing social capital in the form of familial support, including preservation of the cultural orientation of their home country (Gibson, 1988). Relations inside the family would be a strong predictor of how far Latino immigrant children go in school when controlling for the ties that bind a community together, for "[p]arental support leads to higher educational achievement, both directly and indirectly through compensating for the loss of community among migrants" (Portes, 1998: 11).

CONCLUSION

Regardless of a family's immigration status, the educational attainment of parents, and the ties that bind parents of children to other parents in the child's circle of friends, have a positive effect on how far a student will go in school. However, children in native-born households are more positively affected by the density of ties between their parents and their friends' parents, and by their parents' educational attainment, than children in immigrant or combined households. From these findings, I suggest that we need to reframe our conceptions of social capital for the children of immigrants. Evidently, lack of links immigrant parents have with the community do not affect their child's likelihood of continuing on to post-secondary education as much as they do for children of native parents.

One possible reason for this difference between immigrant and native households in the effect of social capital is that family support may be used as a counterweight to the loss of community bonds for immigrant families. In their longitudinal study of adolescents in Toronto, Hagan et al. (1996) confirm Coleman's finding about the deleterious effect of multiple moves on children's emotional adjustment and educational achievement. Leaving a community tends to destroy established bonds, thus depriving family and children of a major source of social capital. These authors find, however, an interaction effect leading to an exacerbation of the loss among children whose parents provide them with weak support, and to a partial neutralization among those in the opposite situation. They find that reduction of social capital in its first form of community social bonds and control is partially compensated by an increase in familial support (Portes, 1998). One negative consequence of tight social controls (or dense ties among community members) is a lack of freedom.

Constraints on individual freedom may be responsible for Rumbaut's (1977) findings that high level of familistic solidarity among recent immigrant students are negatively related to four different educational outcomes, including grades and standardized test scores: "family ties bind, but sometimes these bonds constrain rather than facilitate particular outcomes" (39).

Although the analyses in this chapter don't quite capture the intricacies of how networks and social capital operate within the local community of the immigrant household, these analyses do shed some light on the ways in which human capital and context can affect a child's likelihood to attend some form of post-secondary schooling. For children in immigrant households, there are indeed certain country of origin factors and contextual issues that can affect a child's performance. Previous research would lead us to believe that any immigrant entering the United States without much schooling, and thus a low-status occupation in both the country of origin and in the United States, will most likely raise the child in a depressed community, and thus perpetuate the cycle of poverty (Borjas, 2000). Also, other research has looked to the community in which the immigrant family lives, to foresee how well the children in the family will do in school: if they are in a depressed area they will do poorly (Portes, 1996). I find, however, that even when controlling for the community contact and the availability of role models in an area that a child attends school, children in immigrant households are more likely than children in native households to continue their schooling after high school.

The analyses in this chapter also point to a reconsideration of how parental education affects the educational attainment of youth. For children in native households, parental education has a strong positive relationship to that child's educational attainment, even when language ability, community context, and other social status variables such as occupation are included. For children in immigrant households, however, the relationship between parental educational attainment and child's educational attainment is evident, but not as strong as the effect for native families. I consistently find that immigrant parents' educational attainment does have an effect on a child's likelihood to enter post-secondary school, but that this effect disappears net of occupation, length of time in the United States, or English ability. Yet, the positive relationship between parents' and child's education remains in native households. This does lend some credence to the idea that pre-arrival social status "matters" not only for the economic survival of the immigrant adult, but also for the educational successes of the immigrant adult's child. In sum, we need to consider the role of the parents' and family's social status not only in this country, but also in the country of origin if the parents are foreign-born. In addition, we need to reconsider lumping together children of two-foreign-born parents with children of one-foreign-born parent. Children of combined families have educational trajectories more similar to children in native families than to children in immigrant families.

As demonstrated in Table 3.6, for many of the children in this sample, their ethnicity remains a factor in how far they will go in school, *regardless* of the parents' human capital, the parents' or child's length of time in the United States, or even the parents' or student's stated English proficiency. Chinese students have a higher probability to go farther in school than white students; and Puerto Rican, Mexican, and Filipino students consistently have a lower probability. Could this remaining "ethnicity" effect be because of "culture"? Although these analyses cannot probe the concept of culture for these children, other analyses have. In a study of South East Asian students, Rumbaut & Ima (1988) find similar results: that the children of parents who have a low education or occupational status in country of origin or in the United States, still do very well in school. They attribute the children's excellence in school to the culture of the home—an "intra-family" social capital (Israel, et al., 2001; Glick & White, 2003) that counterbalances any negative effects of language proficiency or lack of familiarity with host culture.

How far children go in school is not simply due to one parental attribute or another, but rather an amalgam of various family circumstances that contribute to the development of the, child's successes. The next chapter investigates the differences in educational attainment that remain for children in certain ethnic groups.

CHAPTER 4

The Influences of Parental Involvement on the Educational Attainment of Children in Immigrant Families

INTRODUCTION

Results in the previous chapter showed that differences in the educational attainment of children of different ethnicities remain, even after considering the human capital of parents, the ethnic capital available in the zip code in which students go to school, and the social capital available in the networks and ties among parents in the student's network of friends. For example, Chinese students of immigrant families are more likely to enter some kind of post-secondary school than are white students in native families; and Puerto Rican, Mexican, Cuban, and Filipino students in immigrant families are less likely to do so. Borrowing from the works of Bourdieu & Passerson (1977) and Annette Lareau (1989), I turn to the role of "culture" to investigate how parenting styles in the home and at school differ for students of different ethnicities and in families of different immigrant status, in order to understand these remaining differences in educational attainment.

Previous research supports the hypothesis that at-home parenting practices and involvement with the school explain much of the variation in school performance based on parents' education (Stevenson & Baker, 1987; Muller, 1993, 1995; Sui-Chi & Willms, 1996), and on race or ethnicity (Duncan, et al., 1998; Garrett, et al., 1994; McNeal, 1999). However, little research has explored the extent of cross-group variation in the relationship between *types* of parent involvement and children's educational attainment (Desimone, 1999), let alone differences by family immigration status.[1] This chapter investigates whether the level of parental involvement in a child's schooling and at home differs by family immigration status, and whether those differences can account for the educational attainment differences among Chinese, Puerto Rican, Mexican, Cuban, Filipino, and white students.

My analyses in this chapter show that immigrant parents have different levels of "involvement" in the schooling of their children. Less-educated immigrant parents, possibly because they are not familiar with the pedagogical techniques or expectations of schools in the United States, tend not to be involved in school-related activities of their children, yet these parents are very much involved in the life of their children at home. I also find that parental supervision at home is a better predictor for a child's educational attainment than is involvement in school activities for children in all family types. In addition, differences between Puerto Rican, Chinese, and white students of immigrant families remain, even when I consider the involvement of parents in school and at home. However, this is not true for Filipino students.

DEFINING CULTURE: PARENTAL INVOLVEMENT IN THE HOME AND AT SCHOOL

The theory of cultural capital (Lareau, 1989) posits that culture can be used as a type of currency to provide students an advantage in schools; culture is considered a family-delivered resource of aspirations, ideologies, manners, and even at-home educational advantages. An understanding of the school process, teacher jargon, and contact with school personnel is a significant determining factor in a child's school performance. Cultural capital works through parents' greater involvement with the child.

Culture is now considered a dominant explanation of achievement differences among different racial and ethnic groups and has been defined in terms of: language proficiency (Cheng, 1987; White & Kaufman, 1997; Wang & Goldschmidt, 1999); norms of appropriate behavior (Ogbu & Simons, 1998; Ogbu, 1990; Hayes, 1992; Fuligni, 1997); social shared cognitive codes and maps and assumptions about worldviews and lifestyle in general (Delgado-Gaitan & Trueba, 1991; Farkas et al., 1990; Farkas, 1996); value-systems of country of origin (Caplan, Choy & Whitmore, 1991); classroom-based differences between teacher and student (Stanic, 1989; Vasquez, 1990; Ray & Poonwassie, 1992; Malloy & Malloy, 1998); and psychological adjustment (Portes, 1999; Kao, 1999).

One branch of research focuses on culture at home to understand why some children go further in school than other children. A second branch focuses on the teacher's interactions with parents and how differences in parental involvement in school affect a teacher's perception of how much a parent cares about the schooling of his or her child, because these in turn may affect student educational attainment. This chapter tests the relative effects of these two conceptions of culture.[2]

Culture as Parenting Style

Researchers often point to differences in home-level characteristics to explain differences in educational attainment by ethnicity, particularly for immigrant families (Wong, 1987; Yao, 1987; Smith & Hausafus, 1998). These theories posit that pre-migration norms and values of immigrant parents are central to understanding ethnic differences in educational achievement (Kim, 2002). Cultural values, beliefs and practices from home countries are transplanted to America and children are socialized into these cultural frames. This framework has often been used to explain the greater academic and economic success for Asians and the lack of academic and economic success for children in Latino immigrant households (Caudill & DeVos, 1956; Caplan et al., 1991; Rutledge, 1992).

However, these theories have been criticized for their sweeping generalizations and failure to consider structural constraints to student success. In their study of the effects of home culture on a student's educational attainment, Steinberg, Dornbusch & Brown (1992) challenge three widely-held explanations for the superior school performance of Asian-American adolescents, and the inferior performance of African- and Latino-American adolescents: first, that parenting practices differ among these groups; second, that Asian parents value education more than the parents from these other groups

do; and third, that black and Latino students are more negative about
the occupational rewards of academic success.

Their findings counter the differential cultural values hypothesis
that ethnic differences in achievement can be explained in terms of the
value placed on education. They find that African-American and Latino
students are just as likely as other students to believe that education is
important for their life chances, as are their parents. Furthermore,
parents of white and Latino children are more potent sources of
influence than are parents of Asian-American or African-American
youngsters. Asian-American and African-American students are more
influenced by their peers, and less by their parents, in matters of
academic achievement than are white or Latino students: although
parents are the most salient influence on youngsters' long-term
educational plans; peers are the most potent influence on their day-to-
day behaviors in school (e.g., how much time they spend on homework,
whether they enjoy coming to school each day, and how they behave in
the classroom).

The theory of "Accommodation without Assimilation" (Gibson,
1988; Ghuman, 1997), discussed in Chapter One, also counters the
traditional explanations for how culture affects schooling success. This
theory suggests that students who are more connected to their parents'
home country culture and value system, and thus less integrated into
their mainstream peer group's adolescent value system, go farther in
school. Parental supervision of the child's activities in the home
(whether it be who the child spends time with, or how the child spends
his or her time) is a factor in determining the child's educational
attainment. The case studies that this theory has been applied to include
Punjabi Sikh (Gibson, 1988) and Mexican (Suarez-Orozco, 1991)
families.

The transference of cultural mores and values from parent to child
is one form of parental involvement that can affect a child's educational
attainment. Another is the parents' involvement in their child's school.

Culture as a Tool: Teacher-Parent Gaps in Perception of Involvement

In her study of parental involvement in the schooling of first grade
children, Lareau (1989) found that there was a disjunction between how
parents and teachers interpreted the parents' concern for their child's

schooling. Less-educated parents were less likely than more-educated parents to voice opinions to teachers or to appear directly involved in assisting their children with learning material. Less-educated parents were not comfortable questioning the teaching practices of their child's teacher because he or she represented an authority figure—one who was responsible for the schooling of their child. In addition, less-educated parents were not as able to assist their children in the mastery of content because they themselves were not familiar with the material. If the teacher does not see the parent involved in school activities, the teacher is likely to assume that the child is disengaged with school because there is no support at home; consequently, their expectations for the child decline.

As detailed in Chapter One, immigrant parents face a unique set of obstacles in becoming involved in their child's schooling. Many do not have many years of formal schooling. Lack of language skills may impede an immigrant parent's communication with a teacher or involvement in their child's school activities. Additionally, in many of the source countries from which present immigrants derive, school and home are two separate realms. The teacher is in charge of ensuring the education of the child; the parent is in charge of ensuring that the child attends school.

Teachers in the United States assume that parents who care about a student's schooling will be involved: whether physically in activities at school, in communication with the teacher, or at home assisting with studying. The teacher's perception of the involvement of a parent may translate into whether the teacher believes that the parent cares about the schooling of the child. Teachers act as "gatekeepers" (Lamont & Lareau, 1988), holding the keys to upward advancement of students. Gatekeepers and other authority figures recognize and reward a broad list of characteristics, including habits, skills, and styles as well as attitudes, preferences, knowledge, goods, and credentials. Following on the theoretical premises of Bourdieu & Passerson (1977), Farkas (1996) argues that society is composed of status groupings, each with its own status culture controlling access to the rewards and privileges of group membership. There is a cultural hegemony of middle and upper status grouping that operates through school and the workplace. Schools become a cultural battleground within which minority and poverty group children are fundamentally disadvantaged. Parental skills, habits, and styles determine the very early cognitive skills of their children.

These influence the child's habits and styles via his or her estimation of the success they can expect from hard effort at tasks that require and increase cognitive skills. Thus, skills, habits, and styles are central to stratification outcomes formed at a young age, and essentially without conscious intent on the children's part. At the macro-level, gatekeepers (in this case, school teachers) as well as peer group and parental preferences and practices, define reward structures. At the micro-level, individuals respond to these reward structures with strategies of action determined by their access to differentially valued cultural resources. Parenting style and the perception of low parental involvement by teachers can each have a deleterious effect on how far through school a student advances.

Based on this body of research, we would expect that culture, however defined or conceptualized, could influence the educational attainment of a child above and beyond the typical predictors of parents' social status or the available social resources in the community. Culture, then, may be the reason why students from Chinese, Mexican, Filipino, Cuban, and Puerto Rican backgrounds have such different schooling outcomes from children of other ethnicities.

RESEARCH QUESTIONS AND HYPOTHESES

Two questions guide the analyses in this chapter. First, do parenting styles in the home and parental involvement in school vary by ethnicity or family's immigration status? I expect immigrant families to have less communication with their children about their studies or activities in school and to have less contact with school personnel and less involvement in activities in the child's school for four reasons. One, if the parents do not speak English very well, they may not feel comfortable visiting the school or know what topics the child is studying in school. Two, as Lareau's (1989) findings about social class differences in parental involvement describe, if the newly-arriving parents do not have a high amount of education, they may feel uncomfortable talking to teachers or counselors, or know about what their child is studying in school. Three, in addition to language difficulties or the interaction with education, immigrant parents may not be comfortable communicating with their child about school activities because they are not accustomed to the educational practices and culture of schools in the United States. Many parents do not realize that teachers expect them to be involved in the lives of their children in school. Instead, they might consider their involvement as a sign that the teacher is not competent in his or her job. Four, a newly-arrived immigrant may not yet have a system of connections within the community to be able to understand the schooling practices of their child's school and what is expected from them as parents.

For those immigrant adults who do not have language difficulties, who are not attached to previous country of origin conceptions of authority of the teacher, and who do have the networks or know how to maneuver through school for their children, lack of interest may explain lack of involvement in their child's schooling. In order to see if parental involvement in home and at school differs among the students, I examine differences in involvement of parents for children of different ethnicities and immigration status.

Second, does the parenting style at home or involvement in school affect a child's post-secondary education? If differences in parental involvement at home or at school exist among the ethnic groups or by family's immigration status, it is important to see whether these differences affect how well students move through school. If the coefficients for parental involvement at home and in school are a positive determinant for the schooling success of a child in an immigrant family when controlling for the family's time in United States, language ability, social ties within community, and country of origin, then involvement in the life of the child at home and in school are significant factors beyond assimilation of the immigrant family in determining how far in school a child goes.

DATA AND ANALYTIC MODELS

I use student and parent responses to questions about parental involvement at home and at school from the base year (1988) through third follow-up (1994) of the National Educational Longitudinal Study. As in the previous chapter, I match information about the proportion of upper-middle class students in the zip code of the school from the 1990 U.S. Census STMP3 zip code files.

I use three indicators to measure parental involvement for the students in the sample: 1) communication between the child and parent about school activities, programs and what the student studies; 2) parental supervision of the child's behavior at home, such as checking homework or requiring that chores be done; and 3) parental interaction with school personnel or involvement in activities at the child's school. Communication is important because it is through active parent-child communication that the importance of schooling and education can be conveyed to the child (McNeal, 1999). Supervision at home, could positively affect educational attainment because parents who closely monitor their children's behavior may well have a great investment in the child's educational performance (Coleman, 1987; Singh et al., 1995; McNeal, 1999). Parents' direct involvement with the school is often the only behavior seen by teachers or administrators. I operationalize these three indicators with six variables:

- Child's perception of parent-student communication
- Parent's perception of parent-student communication
- Child's perception of parent supervision at home
- Parent's perception of parent supervision at home
- Child's perception of parents' involvement in school-related activities
- Parent's perception of their involvement in school-related activities

I use a standardized index when I construct variables from two or more survey questions. The other variables are scales based on the responses of one survey question. Appendix F shows how I construct each variable that measures parental involvement.

To answer my first research question, I use these six parental involvement variables as dependent variables in ordinary least square regression analysis to investigate whether parental involvement differs by ethnic group, immigration status, or the network ties that bind a community together. To answer my second research question, I use ordered logistic regression analysis to investigate how parental involvement variables affect subsequent years of schooling for eighth graders based on ethnicity and family immigration status. I control for language ability of the parents, whether a foreign parent arrived recently to the United States, age of the parents, educational attainment of parents, and social capital ties. I also include the index of upper-middle class residents in the school's zip code and whether the family lives in an urban area, to control for any contextual effects. Other controls are whether the child arrived in the United States in the last five years, the grade the child started school in the U.S. (kindergarten if native-born), whether the child is limited English proficient (LEP), and gender of the child.

PARENTAL INVOLVEMENT DIFFERENCES BY ETHNICITY, IMMIGRATION STATUS, AND EDUCATIONAL ATTAINMENT OF PARENTS

Table 4.1 presents mean differences for the three parental involvement indicators by race and ethnicity, family immigration status, parents' education level, parents' English ability, and level of social capital. This table also shows the differences for the child's post-secondary education choices. The columns of this table show the differences between child and parent responses regarding the level of communication between parents and children about school-related activities and experiences, supervision at home, and parents' involvement at school.

Table 4.1: One-way Analysis of Variance of Mean Differences in Perceptions of Parent-Student Communication, Supervision at Home, and Parental Involvement at School

	Communication		Supervision		Involvement	
	Child	Parent	Child	Parent	Child	Parent
Overall	2.041	2.726	1.953	0.001	1.915	0.001
	(0.761)	(0.509)	(0.611)	(0.548)	(1.097)	(0.566)
Child's Post-Secondary Education in 1994						
Did not graduate from high school	2.057	2.730	1.949	-0.027	1.899	0.016
	(0.759)	(0.513)	(0.621)	(0.556)	(1.085)	(0.576)
No post-secondary education	2.052	2.710	1.939	0.004	1.916	0.006
	(0.754)	(0.524)	(0.609)	(0.541)	(1.101)	(0.583)
Two year-degree institution	2.023	2.739	1.962	-0.006	1.908	-0.007
	(0.763)	(0.489)	(0.617)	(0.563)	(1.091)	(0.550)
Four year-degree institution	2.047	2.718	1.955	0.021	1.930	0.002
	(0.765)	(0.514)	(0.603)	(0.534)	(1.106)	(0.567)
Between Group F=	4.13±	1.710	3.86±	5.72*	0.700	0.130

(continued on next page)

Table 4.1: (continued)

	Communication		Supervision		Involvement	
	Child	Parent	Child	Parent	Child	Parent
Race/ Ethnicity						
White	2.049	2.721	1.955	0.007	1.908	-0.027
	(0.757)	(0.508)	(0.610)	(0.543)	(1.103)	(0.546)
Black	2.053	2.715	1.928	-0.037	1.944	0.131
	(0.746)	(0.534)	(0.615)	(0.567)	(1.058)	(0.643)
Mexican	2.011	2.803	1.952	-0.058	1.893	0.110
	(0.768)	(0.443)	(0.614)	(0.594)	(1.118)	(0.622)
Puerto Rican	1.965	2.701	1.926	-0.052	1.868	-0.029
	(0.797)	(0.600)	(0.608)	(0.586)	(1.040)	(0.556)
Cuban	1.968	2.667	1.958	-0.014	1.916	-0.018
	(0.808)	(0.618)	(0.599)	(0.486)	(1.145)	(0.450)
Chinese	2.052	2.675	1.934	0.090	2.071	-0.139
	(0.839)	(0.625)	(0.639)	(0.476)	(1.150)	(0.477)
Filipino	2.139	2.766	2.143	0.127	1.860	-0.045
	(0.722)	(0.464)	(0.543)	(0.549)	(1.166)	(0.480)
South East Asian	2.952	2.657	2.015	0.036	1.918	-0.048
	(0.835)	(0.518)	(0.597)	(0.515)	(1.158)	(0.481)
Korean	1.979	2.706	1.926	0.014	1.949	0.165
	(0.756)	(0.572)	(0.643)	(0.581)	(1.032)	(0.668)
South Asian	2.050	2.554	1.986	0.052	1.944	-0.003
	(0.760)	(0.660)	(0.539)	(0.558)	(1.035)	(0.525)
Pacific Islander	2.226	2.803	1.922	0.070	1.851	-0.043
	(0.636)	(0.452)	(0.633)	(0.475)	(0.925)	(0.652)
Japanese	2.059	2.846	1.948	-0.023	2.084	-0.101
	(0.752)	(0.352)	(0.634)	(0.552)	(1.138)	(0.618)
Between Group $F=$	1.050	2.95*	1.020	1.71	0.80	12.06*
Family's Immigration Status						
Immigrant	2.012	2.711	1.960	0.007	1.904	-0.013
	(0.791)	(0.524)	(0.616)	(0.573)	(1.138)	(0.530)
Combined	2.029	2.748	1.944	0.025	1.861	0.051
	(0.782)	(0.503)	(0.622)	(0.510)	(1.086)	(0.586)
Native	2.047	2.724	1.954	-0.002	1.925	0.215
	(0.754)	(0.566)	(0.609)	(0.552)	(1.094)	(0.407)
Between Group $F=$	1.67	1.10	0.23	3.61^{+}	$4.84\pm$	$5.57\pm$

(continued on next page)

Table 4.1: (continued)

	Communication		Supervision		Involvement	
	Child	Parent	Child	Parent	Child	Parent
Parents' Years of Schooling						
Less than high school	2.007	2.722	1.931	-0.006	1.929	0.018
	(0.769)	(0.524)	(0.640)	(0.545)	(1.128)	(0.587)
High School Graduate	2.063	2.737	1.943	-0.004	1.910	0.014
	(0.761)	(0.502)	(0.618)	(0.551)	(1.104)	(0.566)
Some College or College Degree	2.032	2.720	1.956	0.004	1.093	-0.003
	(0.758)	(0.510)	(0.603)	(0.555)	(1.087)	(0.480)
Post-BA	2.043	2.725	1.970	0.000	1.936	-0.025
	(0.775)	(0.505)	(0.606)	(0.522)	(1.096)	(0.567)
Between Group F=	2.14	2.71[+]	2.34	2.37	0.55	1.54
Parents' English Ability						
Fluent	2.044	2.719	1.951	0.001	1.919	-0.001
	(0.756)	(0.514)	(0.612)	(0.550)	(1.097)	(0.567)
Not Fluent	2.027	2.749	1.974	-0.006	1.905	0.004
	(0.787)	(0.494)	(0.608)	(0.553)	(1.103)	(0.566)
Between Group F=	0.22	7.02	0.44	0.15	0.05	0.21
Parents Know Child's Friends' Parents						
None	2.027	2.693	1.963	0.017	1.894	-0.005
	(0.753)	(0.530)	(0.621)	(0.545)	(1.097)	(0.554)
Many or Some	2.056	2.744	1.949	-0.005	1.920	-0.005
	(0.763)	(0.483)	(0.614)	(0.549)	(1.093)	(0.553)
Between Group F=	1.27	5.04±	2.21	4.34±	0.82	3.01

Sources: Student and Parent files of the National Education Longitudinal Study (1988-1994) and 1990 U.S. Census (STMP3 zip code files)

Notes: Standard deviations in parenthesis

Weights to adjust for sampling probability used

[+]p<.05,±p<.01*p<.001

A child's post-secondary education in 1994 is positively associated with a student's eighth grade response about parental communication about school ($F=4.13$, $p<.01$) and both the child and the parent responses of parental supervision at home ($F=3.86$, $p<.01$ for students and $F=5.72$, $p<.001$ for parents). Student perceptions of parent-student communication about the student's experiences in school don't appear to differ significantly for children of different ethnic sub-groups, but parent perceptions do differ (F=1.05 for student responses; F=2.95, p<.001, for parent responses).

Mexican parents report the highest mean levels of frequency of communication with their children (2.80 out of 3.00). South Asian parents report the lowest level of communication with their children (2.55 out of 3.00).[3] Since Mexican-descent students have the lowest educational attainment among all children of different ethnic sub-groups, these parental responses about communication are negatively associated with child's post-secondary schooling progress: The more communicative a parent says they are with their child, the less far the child goes in school. However, the parental question about communication does not focus on the student's academic or disciplinary problems in school, but rather about a child's experiences as a whole so it is difficult to ascertain the reasons for a parent's communication with their child.

The last column of Table 4.1 shows that ethnic groups also differ on parent perceptions about their involvement in school (F=12.06, p<.001). This is not the case for the student's perspective on involvement of their parents in school. What is most striking about the parent perspectives of their own involvement is that black and Mexican parents have the relatively high mean reports of their own involvement in school activities (0.131 and 0.110, respectively), yet the children in these racial and ethnic groups, in general, do not go as far in school as the other groups. Chinese parents, whose children go the farthest in school, have the lowest self-report of involvement in school (-0.139). Again, the opposite of what we would expect occurs for these ethnic groups: there is a negative relationship between child's educational attainment and the involvement of the parent.

According to the parental responses in the fifth column, parents supervise their children less at home in native families than in immigrant families. Yet, native parents claim that they are much more involved in school activities than parents in immigrant families claim (F=5.57, p<.01). Both the child's and the parents' responses for parental communication, supervision, and involvement based on the English fluency of the parent are not significantly different from each other.

Further down Table 4.1 are differences in parent-student communication, supervision at home, and parental involvement based on the social ties parents have with the parents in their child's peer group. Based on social ties, children do not believe that their parents are any more or less communicative, supervisory at home, or involved in school. There is also not any significant difference in parent response about involvement at school based on how many of the parents in their child's circle of friends they know.

While informative, these mean differences do not tell us whether the above differences in parent-student communication at home, parental supervision at home, or parental involvement, remain when controlling for a parent's English ability, their length of time in the U.S., or the community context of the family. In order to fully answer my first research question about whether families of different ethnicity or immigration status are involved at home and in school differently, I turn to ordinary least square regressions to examine the relative effects of each variable.

Table 4.2 examines the effects of ethnicity, parents' education, parents' English ability, and community context on parent-student communication about school-related material and activities, by family's immigration status. Table 4.3 does the same for parents' supervision at home. Table 4.4 looks at student and parent responses of how involved the parent is in the child's school. For ease of analysis, only the ethnicities of students with large enough sample sizes are shown: black, Mexican, Puerto Rican, Cuban, Chinese, and Filipino students. The reference group is white students.

As Table 4.2 shows, very few variables have an effect on a child or parent response about the communication within their family about school. It is worth noting that the R^2 in each of these models is very close to zero: the variables that one would assume help to explain communication about school at home do not, in fact, have a significant effect on communication from either the child's or the parent's perspective. Nonetheless, the patterns we see here are worth noting.

The index of upper-middle class residents in the school's zip code has a positive effect on an immigrant family child's response. The higher the index, the more often the family communicates about school, according to the child. These same effects are not apparent for the parents' perspective of communication about school at home.

Table 4.2: Ordinary Least Square Regression Analyses of Student and Parent Response of Communication about School at Home

Dependent variable = Parent-Student Communication about School

	Immigrant		Combined		Native	
	Student response	Parent response	Student response	Parent response	Student response	Parent response
R^2	0.046	0.065	0.118	0.083	0.006	0.003
Constant	2.314*	2.880*	3.263*	2.797*	2.061*	2.786*
	(0.383)	(0.192)	(0.609)	(0.326)	(0.210)	(0.114)
Black	0.066	-0.193	0.597±	-0.063	-0.024	0.026
	(0.174)	(0.125)	(0.212)	(0.100)	(0.039)	(0.022)
Mexican	-0.023	-0.024	-0.363	0.037	0.049	0.061
	(0.220)	(0.068)	(0.196)	(0.059)	(0.051)	(0.031)
Puerto Rican	-0.099	-0.005	-0.348	-0.092	-0.337	-0.084
	(0.209)	(0.101)	(0.303)	(0.089)	(0.230)	(0.189)
Cuban	-0.276	-0.118	0.173	-0.115	0.110	0.082
	(0.191)	(0.145)	(0.344)	(0.420)	(0.286)	(0.148)
Chinese	0.065	-0.109	0.155	0.223	-0.397	0.102
	(0.166)	(0.093)	(0.214)	(0.175)	(0.218)	(0.059)
Filipino	-0.375	-0.040	0.154	0.075	-0.101	0.248*
	(0.198)	(0.074)	(0.202)	(0.076)	(0.357)	(0.033)

(continued on next page)

Table 4.2: (continued)

	Immigrant		Combined		Native	
	Student response	Parent response	Student response	Parent response	Student response	Parent response
Parents' Education	-0.0005	-0.003	-0.004	0.004	0.006	0.001
	(0.015)	(0.007)	(0.019)	(0.014)	(0.004)	(0.003)
Parents' English	-0.040	-0.003	-0.123	0.018	-0.002	-0.021
	(0.035)	(0.019)	(0.065)	(0.037)	(0.038)	(0.107)
Parents know child's friends' parents	-0.008	-0.010	0.092	-0.073	-0.051⁻	-0.015
	(0.175)	(0.042)	(0.125)	(0.053)	(0.025)	(0.015)
Index of upper-middle class	0.118±	0.015	-0.015	-0.092	-0.020	0.001
	(0.039)	(0.022)	(0.153)	(0.074)	(0.013)	(0.010)
in zip code	(0.032)	(0.070)	(0.130)	(0.097)	(0.025)	(0.020)
N=	934		434		8220	

Sources: Student and Parent Files of the National Education Longitudinal Study (1988-1994) and 1990 U.S. Census (STMP3 zip code files)

Notes: Huber White/ Sandwich standard errors in parentheses

Weights to account for probability of being sampled employed

Models control for parents' age and time in the U.S., urban and rural

⁻p<.05, ±p<.01, * p<.001

Table 4.3: Ordinary Least Square Regression Analyses of Students and Parent Responses of Supervision at Home

Dependent variable = Parent Supervision at Home

	Immigrant		Combined		Native	
	Student response	Parent response	Student response	Parent response	Student response	Parent response
R^2	0.036	0.036	0.062	0.077	0.003	0.003
Constant	2.148*	0.049	2.220*	-0.469	1.806*	-0.177
	(0.288)	(0.303)	(0.486)	(0.269)	(0.181)	(0.178)
Black	0.202	0.002	0.197	-0.093	0.005	0.002
	(0.139)	(0.144)	(0.190)	(0.153)	(0.038)	(0.033)
Mexican	-0.042	0.059	-0.125	-0.033	0.088	-0.063
	(0.115)	(0.130)	(0.128)	(0.083)	(0.044)	(0.045)
Puerto Rican	-0.010	-0.090	0.124	0.085	0.089	-0.017
	(0.115)	(0.173)	(0.147)	(0.132)	(0.110)	(0.164)
Cuban	-0.010	0.185	0.433$^+$	-0.103	0.103	0.273$\pm$
	(0.187)	(0.162)	(0.170)	(0.147)	(0.168)	(0.078)
Chinese	-0.100	0.241*	-0.072	0.248	-0.198	-0.066
	(0.127)	(0.117)	(0.166)	(0.145)	(0.174)	(0.140)
Filipino	0.274*	0.215	0.272	0.081	0.223	0.194
	(0.106)	(0.149)	(0.141)	(0.110)	(0.174)	(0.198)

(continued on next page)

Table 4.3: (continued)

	Immigrant		Combined		Native	
	Student response	Parent response	Student response	Parent response	Student response	Parent response
Parents' Education	-0.010	-0.017	-0.015	0.040±	0.003	0.004
	(0.011)	(0.011)	(0.017)	(0.015)	(0.004)	(0.005)
Parents' English	0.006	0.026	-0.059	-0.019	0.010	-0.002
	(0.029)	(0.025)	(0.039)	(0.025)	(0.029)	(0.021)
Parents know child's friends' parents	-0.092	-0.108	0.044	-0.128	-0.014	-0.015
	(0.055)	(0.056)	(0.088)	(0.072)	(0.022)	(0.021)
Index of upper-middle class in zip code	0.028	0.005	0.097⁻	-0.055	0.016	-0.010
	(0.028)	(0.027)	(0.043)	(0.041)	(0.012)	(0.010)
N=	934		434		8220	

Sources: Student and Parent Files of the National Education Longitudinal Study (1988-1994) and 1990 U.S. Census (STMP3 zip code files)

Notes: Huber White/ Sandwich standard errors in parentheses

        Weights to account for probability of being sampled employed

        Models control for parents' age and time in the U.S., rural, and urban

⁻p<.05, ± p<.01, * p<.001

Table 4.4: Parent and Student Responses of Parental Involvement in School

Dependent variable = Parental Involvement in Child's School

	Immigrant		Combined		Native	
	Student response	Parent response	Student response	Parent response	Student response	Parent response
R^2	0.057	0.072	0.049	0.083	0.002	0.025
Constant	2.089*	-0.463[+]	2.221±	-0.853[+]	2.197*	-0.313
	(0.480)	(0.191)	(0.791)	(0.366)	(0.303)	(0.197)
Black	0.304	0.321[+]	0.060	-0.084	0.072	0.166*
	(0.270)	(0.164)	(0.353)	(0.166)	(0.071)	(0.044)
Mexican	0.500±	0.394*	-0.147	0.249±	-0.051	0.132±
	(0.163)	(0.081)	(0.216)	(0.087)	(0.081)	(0.042)
Puerto Rican	0.496	0.201[+]	-0.092	0.343[+]	-0.286	-0.112
	(0.293)	(0.081)	(0.327)	(0.169)	(0.277)	(0.104)
Cuban	0.689±	0.206	-0.020	0.351	-0.286	0.170
	(0.248)	(0.109)	(0.440)	(0.274)	(0.250)	(0.150)
Chinese	0.470±	0.031	0.146	-0.062	-0.308	0.100
	(0.165)	(0.077)	(0.341)	(0.171)	(0.263)	(0.155)
Filipino	0.380	0.122	0.172	0.073	0.384	-0.393[+]
	(0.197)	(0.083)	(0.215)	(0.123)	(0.485)	(0.192)

(continued on next page)

Table 4.4: (continued)

	Immigrant		Combined		Native	
	Student response	Parent response	Student response	Parent response	Student response	Parent response
Parents' Education	-0.009	0.004	-0.018	-0.002	0.005	-0.002
	(0.019)	(0.008)	(0.031)	(0.015)	(0.008)	(0.004)
Parents' English	-0.024	0.008	0.016	0.111	-0.054	0.018
	(0.047)	(0.022)	(0.074)	(0.043)	(0.047)	(0.027)
Parents know child's friends'	-0.250⁺	-0.027	-0.159	0.045	0.002	-0.022
parents	(0.115)	(0.054)	(0.151)	(0.071)	(0.038)	(0.022)
Index of upper-middle class	0.047	-0.009	0.085	0.013	-0.024	0.040*
in zip code	(0.058)	(0.029)	(0.085)	(0.036)	(0.022)	(0.010)
N=	934		434		8220	

Sources: Student and Parent Files of the National Education Longitudinal Study (1988-1994) and 1990 U.S. Census (STMP3 zip code files)

Notes: Huber White/ Sandwich standard errors in parentheses

Weights to account for probability of being sampled employed

Models control for parents' age and time in the U.S., rural, and urban

⁺p<.05, ±p<.01, * p<.001

Black combined families are more likely than white combined families to communicate about school at home, according to the child, even when considering the parents' educational attainment and English ability, or the community context. Ethnic differences in communication about school also exist for Native families. Filipino families, in particular, are more likely than white native families to communicate about school. Yet, this is according to the parents and not the children. All other children and parents are not more or less likely than their white native family peers to feel that their parents are more communicative.

Table 4.3 examines the perceptions of adult supervision at home by immigration status. Across the three types of families, the educational attainment of parents, the social ties, and index of upper-middle class residents, do not affect the child or parent perceptions of adult supervision at home for immigrant or native families. For combined families, however, parental education has a positive effect on a parent's perception of amount of supervision the child has at home, as does the index of upper-middle class adults in the zip code.

In Table 4.3, parent and child responses of supervision in the home vary somewhat by race/ethnicity, although there are few statistically significant coefficients. Chinese immigrant parents claim, more so than do white parents, to supervise their children more at home, but their children do not feel that their parents supervise them any more than their white counterparts feel their parents do. The opposite is the case for Filipino immigrant families. In combined families, Cuban children claim, more so than do white children, their parents supervise them. Yet, in native families, it is the Cuban parents who state, more so than do white native parents, that they supervise their children

Table 4.4 further demonstrates how different the perceptions about parental involvement of a child and parent are. For immigrant families, parents of black and Mexican and Puerto Rican children see themselves as more involved in school, than do the parents of white children, even when controlling for their educational attainment and English ability or community context. This is also the case for combined and native Mexican families. Mexican students in immigrant families tend to agree with their parents: they respond that their parents are more involved in their schooling, as compared to the responses within a white immigrant family. Chinese and Cuban parents are also more involved than white parents in their child's school, according to the students. Only for immigrant families do more non-white students than white students respond that their parents are more involved in their school. There is no significant difference among ethnic groups in a student's response about the involvement of their parents in school. There is some diversity in how involved a parent feels he or she is by ethnicity for native families. In addition to Mexican parents mentioned above, black parents also feel that they are involved in their child's school, even when controlling for educational attainment and English ability, or community context and social ties. Filipino parents, however, are less involved in their child's schooling than are white parents, according to parents, even when controlling for their educational attainment and English ability or community context and social ties.

It is clear that parents and children have differing views about the level of communication at home about school experiences, supervision at home, or involvement in school-related activities. There are differences in parental involvement by ethnicity, immigration status, and language ability. Yet, for all of the measures of parental involvement, parents' years of schooling does not have an effect apart from the other variables effects; a combined-family parent's response of supervision being the exception.

THE EFFECTS OF PARENTAL INVOLVEMENT ON STUDENTS' POST-SECONDARY EDUCATION

The analyses in Tables 4.5 examine how the three conceptions of parental involvement affect, both separately and together, the student's post-secondary schooling choices in 1994 for immigrant, combined, and native families. In these analyses I perform ordered logistic regressions to examine the odds of a child moving from one category of post-secondary schooling to another. Post-secondary schooling is measured with the same four categories as in Chapter Three:

0. Not a high school graduate
1. High school graduate, no post-secondary education
2. High school graduate, entered a two-year associates or vocational degree program
3. High school graduate, entered a four-year bachelor's degree program.

Model 1 examines the effects of ethnicity, parents' educational attainment and English ability, social ties and community context, on a child's post-secondary education. Models 2 and 3 show how parent-student communication at home about school events and experiences, whether from the child or the parents' perception, affects the student's post-secondary schooling choices. Models 4 and 5 show the effects of student and parent perceptions of parental supervision at home on the child's post-secondary schooling. Models 6 and 7 show the effects for student and parent perceptions of parental involvement in school. Model 8 uses all six indicators of parental involvement at home and in school. In each of the analyses, I control for the same variables used in Chapter Three: student's age, gender, grade when the child started school in the United States, and whether the student is proficient in English (limited English proficient, or LEP). The complete table is available in Appendix G.

From these analyses, it appears that parental involvement does not explain away any of the differences in how far Chinese or Puerto Rican students go in school compared to white students, as hypothesized. When I control for parent-student communication in Models 2 and 3, parental supervision at home in Models 4 and 5, or for parental involvement at school in Models 6 and 7, or when I combine all six measures of parental involvement in Model 8, Chinese students are still more likely than white students to go farther in school, and Puerto Rican students are still not going to go as far in school as are white students.

Parents' educational attainment has a positive effect on a child's post-secondary schooling decisions for all family type. Likewise, parents' response of their supervision at home has a positive effect on post-secondary education on children of all family types. The one parental involvement indicator that retains any effect on the student's post-secondary schooling choice in Model 8 is the parents' perception of their supervision over the child at home. The more regulations at home and the more assistance a parent offers with the child's homework, the farther in school the child seems to go, net of all other variables.

For immigrant families, English ability remains a significant predictor of a child's decision to continue schooling. For combined families, there are no ethnic differences that affect the child's likelihood to enter post-secondary education.

Table 4.5: Ordered Logistic Regression Analyses of the Effects of Parental Involvement on Post-Secondary Schooling

Dependent variable= Student's Post-Secondary Education Schooling in 1994

	Model 1	Model 2	Model 3	Model 4	Model 5	Model 6	Model 7	Model 8
cut point 1	3.274*	3.201*	3.336*	3.173*	3.265*	3.290*	3.259*	3.072*
	(0.602)	(0.605)	(0.654)	(0.644)	(0.600)	(0.605)	(0.593)	(0.655)
cut point 2	4.718*	4.647*	4.780*	4.617*	4.712*	4.734*	4.705*	4.521*
	(0.609)	(0.612)	(0.66)	(0.652)	(0.609)	(0.612)	(0.600)	(0.664)
cut point 3	6.425*	6.354*	6.487*	6.324*	6.422*	6.441*	6.412*	6.231*
	(0.618)	(0.621)	(0.670)	(0.662)	(0.618)	(0.622)	(0.609)	(0.674)
Both parents foreign-born	2.752⁻	2.598⁺	3.345⁺	2.727⁺	2.749⁻	2.826⁺	2.766⁻	3.320±
	(1.142)	(1.134)	(1.310)	(1.146)	(1.148)	(1.129)	(1.130)	(1.272)
One parent foreign-born	3.165	2.539	2.626	3.188	3.337	3.481	3.467	2.981
	(1.749)	(1.689)	(1.856)	(1.721)	(1.716)	(1.839)	(1.721)	(1.856)
Child's perception of parent-student communication		-0.048						-0.048
		(0.037)						(0.038)
(child: communication * both parents foreign)		0.093						0.124
		(0.124)						(0.131)
(child: communication * one parent foreign)		0.276						0.378
		(0.161)						(0.177)

(continued on next page)

Table 4.5: (continued)

	Model 1	Model 2	Model 3	Model 4	Model 5	Model 6	Model 7	Model 8
Parent's perception of parent-student communication			0.022					-0.024
			(0.056)					(0.056)
(parent: communication * both parents foreign)			-0.192					-0.195
			(0.157)					(0.176)
(parent: communication * one parent foreign)			0.177					0.108
			(0.329)					(0.4132)
Child's perception of parental supervision at home				-0.054				-0.044
				(0.054)				(0.056)
(child: supervision * both parents foreign)				0.015				-0.006
				(0.147)				(0.155)
(child: supervision * one parent foreign)				-0.014				-0.113
				(0.185)				(0.182)
Parent's perception of parental supervision at home					0.154[+]			0.156[+]
					(0.067)			(0.065)
(parent: supervision * both parents foreign)					-0.176			-0.145
					(0.150)			(0.163)
(parent: supervision * one parent foreign)					0.353			0.248
					(0.258)			(0.250)

(continued on next page)

Table 4.5: (continued)

	Model 1	Model 2	Model 3	Model 4	Model 5	Model 6	Model 7	Model 8
Child's perception of parental involvement in school						0.009		0.021
						(0.030)		(0.031)
(child: parental involvement * both parents foreign)						-0.048		-0.072
						(0.087)		(0.090)
(child: parental involvement * one parent foreign)						-0.115		-0.150
						(0.118)		(0.126)
Parent's perception of parental involvement in school							0.043	0.020
							(0.072)	(0.069)
(parent: parental involvement * both parents foreign)							0.074	0.139
							(0.184)	(0.190)
(parent: parental involvement * one parent foreign)							0.295	0.235
							(0.223)	(0.250)
Parents' Education	0.299*	0.299*	0.299*	0.299*	0.299*	0.299*	0.299*	0.299*
	(0.020)	(0.020)	(0.020)	(0.020)	(0.020)	(0.020)	(0.020)	(0.020)
(Education * both parents foreign-born)	-0.228*	-0.228*	-0.229*	-0.228*	-0.228*	-0.227*	-0.228*	-0.230*
	(0.039)	(0.039)	(0.038)	(0.020)	(0.039)	(0.038)	(0.039)	(0.038)
(Education * one parent foreign-born)	-0.034	-0.030	-0.034	-0.034	-0.054	-0.037	-0.037	-0.055
	(0.057)	(0.058)	(0.057)	(0.057)	(0.055)	(0.056)	(0.057)	(0.055)

(continued on next page)

Table 4.5: (continued)

	Model 1	Model 2	Model 3	Model 4	Model 5	Model 6	Model 7	Model 8
Black	-0.113	-0.114	-0.113	-0.115	-0.114	-0.113	-0.119	-0.117
	(0.129)	(0.129)	(0.129)	(0.130)	(0.130)	(0.129)	(0.125)	(0.128)
(Black * both parents foreign-born)	0.453	0.454	0.420	0.461	0.450	0.461	0.421	0.381
	(0.590)	(0.591)	(0.590)	(0.593)	(0.591)	(0.587)	(0.592)	(0.594)
(Black * one parent foreign-born)	-0.270	-0.340	-0.241	-0.250	-0.210	-0.265	-0.224	-0.208
	(0.597)	(0.592)	(0.581)	(0.594)	(0.531)	(0.578)	(0.580)	(0.520)
Mexican	-0.146	-0.147	-0.148	-0.143	-0.137	-0.146	-0.151	-0.134
	(0.160)	(0.160)	(0.150)	(0.160)	(0.161)	(0.160)	(0.160)	(0.161)
(Mexican * both parents foreign-born)	-0.219	-0.212	-0.233	-0.225	-0.230	-0.199	-0.262	-0.281
	(0.381)	(0.380)	(0.382)	(0.380)	(0.382)	(0.381)	(0.373)	(0.373)
(Mexican * one parent foreign-born)	-0.350	-0.250	-0.357	-0.369	-0.356	-0.366	-0.443	-0.341
	(0.474)	(0.439)	(0.472)	(0.472)	(0.476)	(0.472)	(0.483)	(0.444)
Puerto Rican	-1.159[+]	-1.170[+]	-1.155[+]	-1.165±	-1.152±	-1.155[+]	-1.151[+]	-1.161[+]
	(0.453)	(0.459)	(0.452)	(0.453)	(0.447)	(0.453)	(0.452)	(0.453)
(Puerto Rican * both parents foreign-born)	-0.081	-0.071	-0.093	-0.075	-0.093	-0.059	-0.118	-0.097
	(0.716)	(0.722)	(0.715)	(0.716)	(0.716)	(0.726)	(0.715)	(0.724)
(Puerto Rican * one parent foreign-born)	0.168	0.268	0.181	0.182	0.110	0.155	0.074	0.199
	(0.736)	(0.721)	(0.734)	(0.737)	(0.699)	(0.751)	(0.718)	(0.683)

(continued on next page)

Table 4.5: (continued)

	Model 1	Model 2	Model 3	Model 4	Model 5	Model 6	Model 7	Model 8
Cuban	-0.248	-0.242	-0.250	-0.246	-0.267	-0.250	-0.251	-0.263
	(0.346)	(0.349)	(0.344)	(0.351)	(0.334)	(0.345)	(0.341)	(0.340)
(Cuban * both parents foreign-born)	-0.137	-0.137	-0.171	-0.138	-0.115	-0.107	-0.167	-0.166
	(0.536)	(0.537)	(0.539)	(0.540)	(0.699)	(0.538)	(0.529)	(0.534)
(Cuban * one parent foreign-born)	-1.057	-1.165	-0.995	-1.026	-0.964	-1.058	-1.190	-1.124
	(0.871)	(0.882)	(0.885)	(0.890)	(0.828)	(0.834)	(0.918)	(0.875)
Chinese	1.396$^+$	1.390$^+$	1.395$^+$	1.391$^+$	1.420$^+$	1.396	1.402	1.414$^+$
	(0.737)	(0.743)	(0.738)	(0.743)	(0.735)	(0.738)	(0.741)	(0.748)
(Chinese * both parents foreign-born)	0.764	0.782	0.752	0.764	0.744	0.780	0.751	0.757
	(0.875)	(0.880)	(0.879)	(0.877)	(0.871)	(0.876)	(0.80)	(0.888)
(Chinese * one parent foreign-born)	-0.688	-0.710	-0.730	-0.688	-0.837	-0.660	-0.681	-0.822
	(1.189)	(1.217)	(1.184)	(1.190)	(1.194)	(1.170)	(1.195)	(1.196)
Filipino	0.292	0.278	0.288	0.307	0.265	0.295	0.283	0.269
	(0.364)	(0.364)	(0.364)	(0.365)	(0.366)	(0.365)	(0.363)	(0.367)
(Filipino * both parents foreign-born)	-0.406	-0.399	-0.413	-0.408	-0.375	-0.391	-0.416	-0.399
	(0.509)	(0.512)	(0.512)	(0.516)	(0.509)	(0.508)	(0.505)	(0.514)
(Filipino * one parent foreign-born)	-0.166	-0.144	-0.175	-0.167	-0.191	-0.149	-0.171	-0.120
	(0.554)	(0.551)	(0.553)	(0.561)	(0.582)	(0.560)	(0.548)	(0.583)

(continued on next page)

Table 4.5: (continued)

	Model 1	Model 2	Model 3	Model 4	Model 5	Model 6	Model 7	Model 8
Parents know child's friends' parents	1.501*	1.500*	1.501*	1.502*	1.507*	1.501*	1.502*	1.508*
	(0.075)	(0.075)	(0.075)	(0.075)	(0.074)	(0.075)	(0.074)	(0.074)
(parents know many * both parents foreign-born)	-0.924*	-0.919*	-0.921*	-0.930*	-0.933*	-0.937*	-0.922*	-0.933*
	(0.209)	(0.210)	(0.209)	(0.279)	(0.207)	(0.216)	(0.210)	(0.215)
(parents know many * one parent foreign-born)	-0.958±	-0.971*	-0.951±	-0.959±	-0.888±	-0.978±	-0.969*	-0.942±
	(0.278)	(0.273)	(0.276)	(0.279)	(0.276)	(0.285)	(0.273)	(0.272)
Index of upper-middle class in zip code	0.225±	0.224*	0.225*	0.225*	0.227*	0.225*	0.223*	0.226*
	(0.044)	(0.044)	(0.044)	(0.044)	(0.044)	(0.044)	(0.044)	(0.044)
(upper-middle class * both parents foreign-born)	-0.028	-0.031	-0.023	-0.027	-0.029	-0.027	-0.025	-0.026
	(0.104)	(0.104)	(0.104)	(0.104)	(0.104)	(0.104)	(0.103)	(0.103)
(upper-middle class * one parent foreign-born)	-0.028	0.101	0.107	0.098	0.132	0.100	0.093	0.171
	(0.104)	(0.164)	(0.146)	(0.159)	(0.164)	(0.155)	(0.164)	(0.147)

N= 10,547

Sources: Student, Parent, and Teacher Files of the National Education Longitudinal Study (1988-1994) and 1990 U.S. Census (STMP3 zip code files)

Notes: Huber White/ Sandwich standard errors in parentheses

Weights to account for probability of being sampled employed

All models control for urban residence, parents' and child's age, grade when child started school in U.S., gender, and whether child is limited English proficient

+p<.05, ±p<.01, * p<.001

Native Puerto Rican students are less likely than native white students to continue their post-secondary education. Similar to the analyses for immigrant families, parents' educational attainment, social ties, and index of upper-middle class residents in the school's zip code have positive effects on how far a native child goes in school.

CONCLUSIONS

This chapter examined the relationship between parents' attentiveness to the child's activities both within the home and within school by immigration status to explain ethnic differences in likelihood to enter post-secondary schooling. Tables 4.2 through 4.4 show that children of different ethnicities have different perceptions of their parents' involvement in school and at home than their parents do. However, Table 4.5 demonstrates that none of these differences in child or parent perception about parental involvement account for how far the child goes in school by 1994 for immigrant families. Only the parent's perception of their supervision at home has any effect for all children. Evidently, the monitoring of after-school activities around the home and the amount of interest in school-related activities may positively impact the educational attainment of children. From these analyses, the role of parental involvement does not seem to be a large factor in determining the educational attainment of children and does not account for ethnic differences in educational attainment.

CHAPTER 5

Conclusions and Policy Implications

INTRODUCTION

The United States is unlike other major immigrant-receiving nations in that our major policy questions do not center on whether one's bloodline constitutes citizenship or whether to allow for dual citizenship. This is because our conception of citizenship is for the most part based on choice, rather than ancestry. Our central policy concerns regarding immigration focus almost entirely on the economic well-being of our nation: Do immigrants hinder native-born people's economic opportunities? Are immigrants a burden to the economic structure of our labor market? In light of the economic focus of present policy concerns, this study analyzed the intergenerational transmission of status between immigrant adults and their children to answer some of the more vexing questions about today's present immigrant flow.

In the first chapter, I described the general immigrant population in the United States, using various years of the March Current Population Survey and the U.S. Census. From these descriptors, it became clear that present-day immigration is over-represented by people from the Caribbean, Latin America, and Asia. Most recently-arrived immigrants are disproportionately less educated than native-born people in the United States. In addition, because of the lack of educational credentials, the immigrant population overall has a higher poverty rate than the native-born population. From these statistics I turned to analysis of the status attainment patterns for children in immigrant, combined, and native households using data from the 1988-1994 waves of the National Education Longitudinal Study and the Public Use Micro-Samples from the 1990 U.S. Census.

Chapters Two and Three examined the effects of an immigrant adult's educational attainment before arriving to the United States on that adult's economic prospects, in the form of an occupation, and on the child of that adult's potential economic prospects, in the form of their educational attainment. Within these analyses, I included country-level human capital, measured as mean years of schooling from the 2000 Data on Educational Attainment, to ascertain the effects of country of origin human capital differences. I also examined the potential mediating effects of community context, based on the zip code of the public school the child attended in eighth grade, with data from the STMP3 zip code files of the 1990 U.S. Census. In each analysis, I looked to differences among ethnic groups as well as among families with two foreign-born parents, one foreign-born parent, and two native-born parents. As a way to explain differences in post-secondary education choices that remained in immigrant households among Puerto Rican, Chinese, Mexican, Cuban, and Filipino children with their white counterparts, in the final chapter I discuss how involved their parents were at home and at school.

The main goal of this book was to address whether a child of immigrants is destined to follow in the tracks of his or her parents: whether the effects of educational attainment of an immigrant parent on the educational attainment of his or her child are statistically similar to the effects of a native parent's educational attainment on his or her child. By studying the relative effects of educational attainment, I hoped to garner a better understanding of status attainment patterns for children of different ethnicities and of different immigration family types.

Figure 5.1 diagrams the analyses in the book and fleshes out the heuristic diagram provided in Chapter One. Here, I map out the specific variables I used for my analyses and detail the causal patterns. Immigrant adult's post-arrival occupation and student's educational attainment are **bolded** to signify that they are the main dependent variables. All other indicators are independent variables. Note that the arrow between community context and post-arrival social status has two points. This denotes that the causal relationship between the two is unclear and is bi-directional: a family's occupational status could determine the choice of community of a family and the community context could affect the occupational choices available for a family.

Chapter Two examined the first part of the diagram: the effects of pre-arrival educational attainment and country of origin mean levels of education on the post-arrival occupational status of immigrant adults. I controlled for adult characteristics and compared my results for immigrants with natives.

Chapter Three examined the second part of the diagram: the effects of pre-arrival educational attainment and country of origin mean levels of education on the educational attainment of a child. In this chapter, I controlled for parents' and child's characteristics as well as the effects of community context. This chapter compared families with two foreign-born parents and one foreign-born parent to families with two native-born parents.

Chapter Four examined the role of parental involvement to explain any lingering differences among children of different ethnicities that human capital of parents and social capital and ethnic capital of communities did not explain away. Similar to Chapter Three, this chapter also compared families of different immigration type.

Figure 5.1: Linking Immigrant Family Educational Attainment, Occupational Status, and Community Context

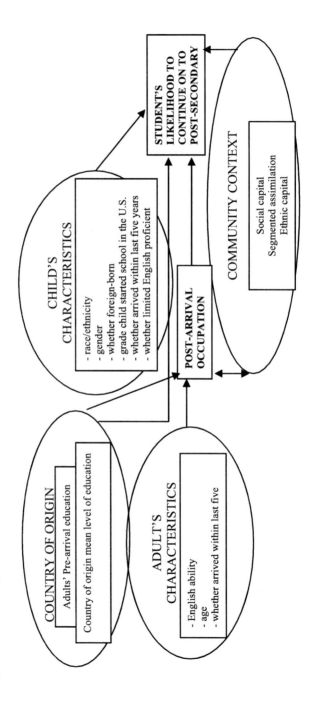

SUMMARY OF FINDINGS

The Role of Educational Attainment

In Chapter Two, I found that for both native and foreign-born adults, educational attainment has a strong and positive effect on that adult's occupational status. Yet this effect is less strong for immigrant than it is for natives. In addition, Chapter Three also found that parents' educational attainment was a clear predictor for a child's likelihood to continue on to post-secondary education in immigrant, combined, and native families. However, that effect is less strong for immigrant families than for native families; and, the effects of educational attainment for combined families are not significantly different from the effects for a native family.

I concluded from these analyses that although educational attainment of a parent is important in predicting their occupational status and how far in school their child will go, it is not the sole determinant for immigrants and their children. To support this conclusion, I compare predicted probabilities of families with less than a high school education in Figure 3.1 to demonstrate that, in general, children of immigrants with less than a high school education are more likely to finish high school and continue on to post-secondary school than both combined and native families with less than a high school education, all else being equal. In fact, children with one foreign-born parent are not significantly more or less likely to continue their education than children with two native parents.

The Role of Social Capital

Of all the community context variables I examined, the one indicator that had any consistent effect on a child's post-secondary schooling choices was the network among a child's parents and the parents in the child's circle of friends. For immigrant, combined, and native families, this measure of social capital was positively associated with a child's schooling choices. Yet, similar to the effects of parents' educational attainment, the effects were relatively stronger for native families than for immigrant families. In addition, the effect of social capital on the student's educational attainment in a combined family was significantly lower than the effect for native families. It is apparent that links among the parents in a student's circle of friends has less of an effect on the schooling choices of that student in an immigrant or combined family, than it does for a student in a native family: within-community ties make a difference for the schooling success of a child of native parents. From these findings, I conclude that the present discussion about the benefits or negative consequences of social capital may be too focused on the native population in the United States, to the detriment of including immigrants. For immigrant and combined families, "weak ties" may offer more of a benefit than strong ties. In addition, immigrants may turn to intra-family connections to compensate for a lack of intra-community connections.

Ethnic Differences

Even when controlling for human capital, community context, and individual-level characteristics, ethnic differences remained in analyses of occupational status of adults and post-secondary schooling choices of children. Puerto Rican students in immigrant and native households were significantly less likely than their white counterparts to continue their post-secondary schooling. Mexican, Cuban, and Filipino students in immigrant households were also less likely than their white counterparts to continue their post-secondary schooling. Chinese students in immigrant households, however, were more likely than their white counterparts to continue post-secondary schooling, net of everything else.

In order to explain these ethnic differences I looked to within-family levels of parental involvement in a child's life at home and at school. My hope was to determine if differences in perceptions of involvement for immigrant and native parents would be the deciding factor in determining a child's decision to stay in school, particularly for the students of the above ethnicities. Of the six parental involvement variables I examined in these analyses, only the supervision by parents at home had any effect on the post-secondary schooling choices of students. None of the remaining indicators had any significant effect on a child's likelihood to continue post-secondary schooling, all else being equal. Theories that use differences in "culture" at home between immigrants and natives or among families of different ethnicities do not bear out in the analyses. Instead, it appears that immigrant, combined, and native families are somewhat similar in their levels of communication about school, supervision at home, and involvement at school, all else being equal. It also appears that none of these indicators of parental involvement, except parents' supervision at home, has a strong effect on the child's post-secondary education choices. For all families with school-age children, the clear message of these analyses is to maintain supervision over students' activities while at home.

POLICY IMPLICATIONS

From the above findings, three major policy implications bear out:

1) Education is important for immigrant and natives to secure a job, but has a weaker effect for immigrants than for natives. This suggests that there is not a straight line between education and occupation for many immigrants. Human capital is an important factor in determining the occupational choices for adults, but factors beyond simply years of school influence an immigrant's post-arrival occupational status once in the United States. This point should be considered if the United States starts to limit entrance into the U.S based on pre-arrival skill level (educational attainment).

2) Education of parents is also important for children's educational choices, yet this effect is weaker for children of two immigrant parents than for children with two native parents. Policy should focus on enabling the children of immigrants to fulfill their potential within the schooling system; they are not confined by their parents' educational attainment to the same extent that children in native households are. Thus, a child with two immigrant parents who have less than a high school degree is not necessarily destined to not complete high school.

3) Ties that bind a family to other families within a network is also an important factor in a child's educational choices, yet is not as strong a factor for children in immigrant or combined households as it is for children in native households. Much attention focuses on the dissolution of community ties (Putnam, 2000), but we should examine the strength of weak ties (Granovetter, 1974), and examine how to enhance the

educational attainment for *all* students via the use of support networks outside a potentially small network of people.

SUGGESTIONS FOR FUTURE RESEARCH

A number of shortcomings in the data I use beg for more research on the topic of status attainment patterns of Latino and Asian children in immigrant households. First, is the use of zip code of the school to define a community. A more appropriate unit of analysis would be the zip code or census tract of a student's *home*, rather than school. However, due to the limitations of the data of the National Education Longitudinal Study, I was only able to retrieve an identification number of a child's school, if it was a public school, from the National Center of Education Statistics and then find the school's zip code from the Common Core of Data. This zip code was thus the smallest unit of analysis I could extract from the community-related 1990 U.S. Census data.

A second shortcoming is the lack of data beyond 1994, only two years after a student finished high school-if they graduated. A fourth wave of NELS using 2000 data is available. However, preliminary analyses show that attrition is very high, particularly for Latino and Asian respondents, making follow-up analyses nearly impossible. These data would have had information on the type of institution a student graduated from and whether the student completed a GED, and would have greatly enhanced these analyses. Rather than postulate about a student's educational attainment, these data would have measured years of schooling directly.

A third shortcoming of the National Education Longitudinal Study is the lack of country of origin indicators for Latinos who are not Mexican, Puerto Rican, or Cuban. This group includes many people from various parts of the Caribbean, Central America, and South America. Students who are South East Asian, South Asian, or Pacific Islanders are also grouped together under a pan-ethnic categorization. Yet, like the grouping of "Latino," these categories consist of a variety of countries that are economically, socially, and culturally different from each other. These analyses would be enhanced greatly with specific country of origin indicators for both Latino and Asians, as well as for the large groupings of "white" and "black."

Beyond the data limitations, a number of avenues for future research abound. One area of interest I have touched upon is the definition of social capital. Although previous research contends that intra-familial social capital is important for immigrants to compensate for any lack of within-community social capital, this fact did not bear out in my examinations of parental involvement. Instead, I found no significant differences on within-family communication about school or life among immigrant, combined, or native families. More research needs to be done on the various conceptions of social capital and how much of the theorizing about social capital that pertain to immigrant or combined families uses native families as the model, even though immigrant and combined families are not affected by social capital in the same way as native families are.

Further research should also examine the role of assimilation on the status attainment process. My analyses consistently found that the children in combined families were not significantly different from native families, yet much previous research on the second generation tends to include children of one foreign-born parent with analyses on children of two foreign-born parents. This is an inaccurate portrayal of the second generation, for combined families are more like native families than they are like immigrant families.

One important area not touched upon in this book is the fact discussed in Chapter One that most immigrants are living not among their co-ethnics, but among fellow immigrants. One could examine where immigrants choose to live, based on their educational attainment or on the connections they have with other recently arrived immigrants. This would show the patterns of settlement within the United States that may have a factor in determining the social capital available within these communities.

A second area not within the scope of the research is the role of gender. Throughout my analyses I found that in all immigrant family types, female children are choosing to continue their schooling beyond high school more than male children are. Although there is a plethora of research on the differences in educational attainment by gender, much of the previous research on female children of immigrant parents suggests that they are less likely than male children of immigrant parents to continue school. This does not seem to be the case with my analyses; more research needs to focus exclusively on female and male children of different ethnicities of different immigrant family types.

In general, there is ample research that still needs to be done on the educational attainment and the inter-generational transmission of status for immigrants and their children. The analyses in this book touch upon some of the more pressing questions, but further research needs to perform longitudinal analyses of within-family mobility, rather than comparing a set of students who are immigrants with a set of students who are the children of one or two immigrants, as previous researchers have done. More systematic research that follows families through time and that separates families with only one foreign-born parent from families with two foreign-born parents would greatly enhance the fields of education and immigration.

Appendix A

Table A.1: Complete List of Mean Levels of Schooling by Country and Gender (adults over age 25)

Ethnicity	Country	Male	Female	Average
"White" (European, Australia, Canada, South Africa, New Zealand)				
	Australia	10.85	10.31	10.57
	Austria	9.66	7.99	8.80
	Belgium	9.08	8.41	8.73
	Canada	11.49	11.38	11.43
	Cyprus	9.22	8.35	8.77
	Denmark	10.97	9.25	10.09
	Finland	10.44	9.86	10.14
	France	8.64	8.14	8.38
	Germany, West	10.22	9.31	9.75
	Greece	9.65	7.46	8.52
	Hungary	9.51	8.21	8.81
	Iceland	9.08	8.43	8.75
	Ireland	9.01	9.02	9.02
	Italy	7.48	6.57	7.00
	Israel	9.40	9.07	9.23
	Malta	7.98	7.18	7.57
	New Zealand	11.80	11.26	11.52
	Netherlands	9.61	8.88	9.24
	Norway	12.14	11.59	11.86
	Poland	10.09	9.74	9.90
	Portugal	5.04	4.80	4.91
	South Africa	8.16	7.58	7.87
	Spain	7.37	7.14	7.25
	Sweden	11.32	11.39	11.36
	Switzerland	11.21	9.59	10.39
	United Kingdom	9.40	9.30	9.35
		9.57	**8.85**	**9.20**

(continued on next page)

Table A.1: (continued)

Ethnicity	Country	Male	Female	Average
"Black" (African or Afro-Caribbean)				
	Algeria	5.74	3.70	4.72
	Benin	3.12	1.13	2.10
	Botswana	5.51	5.21	5.36
	Cameroon	3.83	2.54	3.17
	Central African R.	3.02	1.30	2.11
	Congo	5.17	4.24	4.68
	Gambia	2.65	1.11	1.86
	Ghana	5.11	2.96	4.01
	Kenya	4.72	3.28	3.99
	Lesotho	3.87	5.01	4.47
	Liberia	3.18	1.35	2.26
	Malawi	3.29	1.94	2.58
	Mali	1.10	0.44	0.76
	Mauritius	6.14	4.98	5.55
	Mozambique	1.42	0.98	1.19
	Niger	1.17	0.50	0.82
	Rwanda	2.37	1.70	2.03
	Senegal	2.86	1.61	2.23
	Sierra Leone	2.67	1.36	1.99
	Sudan	2.47	1.35	1.91
	Swaziland	5.33	6.07	5.73
	Togo	4.13	1.60	2.83
	Tunisia	5.14	3.26	4.20
	Uganda	3.39	2.53	2.95
	Zaire	4.55	1.89	3.18
	Zambia	5.91	5.00	5.43
	Zimbabwe	5.88	3.91	4.88
	Barbados	9.06	9.17	9.11
	Haiti	3.04	2.34	2.67
	Jamaica	4.76	5.67	5.22
	Trinidad & Tobago	7.58	7.65	7.62
		4.13	**3.09**	**3.60**
Mexican				
	Mexico	**7.16**	**6.32**	**6.73**

(continued on next page)

Table A.1: (continued)

Ethnicity	Country	Male	Female	Average
Puerto Rican				
	Puerto Rico			**7.00**
Cuban				
	Cuba			**7.23**
"Other Latino" (Latin American or Latin Caribbean)				
	Costa Rica	6.03	6.00	6.01
	Dominican Rep.	5.12	5.22	5.17
	El Salvador	4.56	4.45	4.50
	Guatemala	3.57	2.68	3.12
	Honduras	4.14	4.03	4.08
	Nicaragua	4.05	4.74	4.42
	Panama	7.75	8.05	7.90
	Argentina	8.40	8.57	8.49
	Bolivia	6.19	4.92	5.54
	Brazil	4.62	4.50	4.56
	Chile	7.94	7.85	7.89
	Colombia	4.80	5.21	5.01
	Ecuador	6.74	6.31	6.52
	Guyana	5.97	6.12	6.05
	Paraguay	5.90	5.57	5.74
	Peru	7.97	6.71	7.33
	Uruguay	7.00	7.47	7.25
	Venezuela	5.68	5.55	5.61
		5.91	**5.78**	**5.84**
Chinese				
	China	6.94	4.49	5.74
	Hong Kong	10.09	8.83	9.47
	Taiwan	9.32	7.69	8.53
		8.78	**7.00**	**7.91**
Filipino				
	Philippines	**7.54**	**7.69**	**7.62**
Japanese				
	Japan	**10.13**	**9.34**	**9.72**

(continued on next page)

Table A.1: (continued)

Ethnicity	Country	Male	Female	Average
Korean				
	Korea	**11.54**	**9.42**	**10.46**
South Asian				
	Bangladesh	3.40	1.45	2.45
	India	6.14	3.33	4.77
	Pakistan	3.60	1.21	2.45
	Sri Lanka	6.41	5.79	6.09
		4.89	**2.94**	**3.94**
South East Asian				
	Myanmar (Burma)	2.69	2.21	2.44
	Thailand	6.49	5.73	6.10
		4.59	**3.97**	**4.27**
Pacific Islander				
	Papua New Guinea	2.85	1.90	2.39
	Fiji	8.35	7.58	7.96
		5.60	**4.74**	**5.18**
"Other Race" (Middle Eastern, Central Asian, West Asian, Other Asian)				
	Afghanistan	1.75	0.50	1.14
	Bahrain	6.27	5.81	6.09
	Egypt	6.32	3.76	5.05
	Indonesia	5.39	4.05	4.71
	Iran	5.68	3.63	4.66
	Iraq	5.41	3.25	4.34
	Jordan	8.34	6.35	7.37
	Kuwait	7.19	6.89	7.05
	Malaysia	8.54	7.24	7.88
	Nepal	2.90	0.98	1.94
	Singapore	8.76	7.47	8.12
	Syria	7.12	4.38	5.74
	Turkey	5.64	3.91	4.80
		6.10	**4.48**	**5.30**
Native-born				
	United States	**12.29**	**12.21**	**12.25**

Source: Data on International Educational Attainment (Barro and Lee, 2000)

Appendix B

Table B.1: Variable Descriptions, Means, and Standard Deviations

		1988 NELS N = 27,805		1994 NELS N = 10,547	
		Mean	St. Dev.	Mean	St. Dev.
Schooling Success					
Educational attainment of eighth grader in 1994	0: did not complete high school; no post-secondary schooling 1: completed high school; no post-secondary schooling 2: entered two-year associates or certificate degree program 3: entered four-year bachelor's degree program	N/A	N/A	1.78	1.02
Family Characteristics					
Mother's years of education	min: 6 max: 18 years of schooling	12.90	2.65	11.96	3.23
Father's years of education	min: 6 max: 18 years of schooling	13.53	3.14	12.39	3.67
Parents' years of education	Higher of mother's or father's years of education (corr = 0.568)	13.91	3.09	13.08	3.28
Pre-arrival mother's education	Years of education for immigrant mother	12.11	3.87	11.11	4.17
Pre-arrival father's education	Years of education for immigrant father	13.04	4.27	11.76	4.68
Mother's occupation	Socio-Economic Index Scoring (min: 29.44 max: 64.38)	44.02	12.02	42.15	11.87
Father's occupation	Socio-Economic Index Scoring (min: 29.44 max: 64.38)	44.84	12.42	42.87	11.28
Parents' occupation	Higher of mother's or father's SEI score (corr = 0.366)	45.69	12.62	45.96	12.05
Mother's age	min: 23 max: 54 years old	40.60	6.43	40.41	6.49
Father's age	min: 23 max: 54 years old	43.34	7.08	43.04	7.13
Parents' age	Higher of mother's or father's age (corr = 0.71)	43.19	7.07	42.99	7.09

(continued on next page)

Table B.1: (continued)

		1988 NELS N = 27,805		1994 NELS N = 10,547	
		Mean	St. Dev.	Mean	St. Dev.
Mother's time in U.S.	Mother arrived within last five years (0=No; 1= Yes)	0.012	0.11	0.014	0.12
Father's time in U.S.	Father arrived within last five years (0=No; 1=Yes)	0.013	0.11	0.014	0.11
Parents' time in U.S.	Higher of foreign-born mother's or father's time in U.S. (corr = 0.83)	0.013	0.11	0.014	0.11
Parents' English ability	Index of parents' self-report of ability to speak, read, write, understand English min: 0 max:5 (alpha = 0.99)	4.62	0.96	4.61	1.00
Family's Immigration Status	Native: both parents are native-born (reference) (0=No; 1=Yes)	0.64	0.47	0.77	0.41
	Combined: one parent is foreign-born (0=No; 1=Yes)	0.13	0.33	0.04	0.21
	Immigrant: both parents are foreign-born (0=No; 1=Yes)	0.08	0.28	0.09	0.28
Child's Characteristics					
Child's age	min: 9 max: 18	14.39	0.64	14.42	0.65
Child's time in U.S.	min: 0.5 max: 12	8.13	3.45	8.35	3.24
Child is limited English proficient (LEP)	Child ranks self as having a "low" ability to speak, read, write, understand English or child was in a LEP class in past year (0=No; 1=Yes)	0.20	0.40	0.21	0.40
Generation of child	Third: native-born child w/ native-born parents (reference) (0=No; 1=Yes)	0.63	0.48	0.77	0.41
	Second: native-born child w/ at least one foreign-born parent (0=No; 1=Yes)	0.08	0.27	0.07	0.26
	First: foreign-born child w/ at least one foreign-born parent (0=No; 1=Yes)	0.04	0.21	0.05	0.21

(continued on next page)

Table B.1: (continued)

		1988 NELS N = 27,805		1994 NELS N = 10,547	
		Mean	St. Dev.	Mean	St. Dev.
Race/ Ethnicity	White (reference)	0.58	0.49	0.65	0.47
	Black	0.10	0.31	0.11	0.32
	Mexican	0.07	0.25	0.09	0.29
	Puerto Rican	0.013	0.115	0.009	0.09
	Cuban	0.004	0.069	0.004	0.06
	Other Latino	0.024	0.155	0.023	0.15
	Chinese	0.011	0.105	0.014	0.118
	Filipino	0.010	0.103	0.013	0.116
	Japanese	0.003	0.058	0.004	0.063
	Korean	0.006	0.082	0.009	0.095
	South East Asian	0.008	0.092	0.011	0.105
	South Asian	0.004	0.067	0.005	0.072
	Pacific Islander	0.003	0.058	0.004	0.063
	Other Asian/ Other Ethnicity	0.017	0.131	0.020	0.141

(continued on next page)

Table B.1: (continued)

		1988 NELS N = 27,805		1994 NELS N = 10,547	
		Mean	St. Dev.	Mean	St. Dev.
Segmented Assimilation					
Percent same race/ethnicity	% of householders school's zip code with the same race or ethnicity as 8th grader	53.43	40.48	69.55	35.92
Percent foreign-born	% of householders in school's zip code born outside of U.S.	8.16	11.68	7.29	10.98
Percent recent arrivals	% of foreign-born in school's zip code who arrived between 1987 and 1990	12.07	10.50	11.68	10.90
Residential stability	% of householders in school's zip code who have lived there for min. five years	71.01	13.16	70.41	13.30
Social Capital					
Ties among families	Parents know "some" or "many" of the child's friends' parents (0=No; 1=Yes)	0.30	0.55	0.28	0.45
Index of upper-middle class residents in zip code	standardized composite of:				
	a) proportion of college graduates among persons aged 25 and over				
	b) proportion of employed persons with professional occupations				
	c) median household income				
	min: -1.77 max: 3.91 (alpha 0.93)	0.00	0.94	0.00	0.94

Sources: Student and Parent Files of the National Education Longitudinal Study (1988-1994) and 1990 US Census STMP3 Zip Code Files

Note: Weights to account for sampling probability applied to ethnicity variables

Appendix C

Table C.1 shows the correlations among the family's immigration status, the dependent variables, parents' educational attainment, and the community context variables. As one would expect from the correlation matrices in Chapter Two, family's occupational status is fairly positively associated with parents' educational attainment (r =.562). This relationship is the stronger of any two variables in the table. The percentage of people of the same race in a zip code is negatively associated with having both parents who are foreign-born (r =-.408), but is positively associated with growing up in a native household (r =.448): native families are more inclined to send their children to school in ethnically homogenous areas, relative to foreign families. The opposite relationship is true for the percentage of foreign-born who live in a zip code.

Table C.1: Pairwise Correlations of Dependent Variables with Parents' Educational Attainment and Community Context

	1	2	3	4	5	6	7	8	9	10	11	12
1. Both parents are foreign-born	1.000											
2. One parent is foreign-born	-.068	1.000										
3. Both parents are native-born	-.590	-.411	1.000									
4. Educational attainment in 1994	.086	.010	.001	1.000								
5. Family occupation	-.033	.003	.098	.329	1.000							
6. Parents' educational attainment	-.080	.015	.115	.376	.562	1.000						
7. % same race/ ethnicity in zip code	-.408	-.144	.432	.015	.068	.070	1.000					
8. % foreign in zip code	.448	.130	-.451	.009	-.053	-.116	-.324	1.000				
9. % of recently arrived foreign in zip code	.164	.055	-.168	.001	.005	-.020	-.238	.345	1.000			
10. % with same residence for last five years	.100	.212	-.101	.031	.024	.012	-.055	.187	-.032	1.000		
11. Urban	.160	.038	-.175	-.032	-.039	-.045	-.211	.306	.167	.233	1.000	
12. Parents know child's friends' parents	-.058	-.024	.108	.359	.154	.182	.109	-.109	-.060	-.054	-.111	1.000
13. Index of upper-middle class in zip code	.103	.057	-.073	.242	.279	.329	-.057	.104	.096	.176	-.022	.063

Sources: Student and Parent Files of the National Education Longitudinal Study (1988-1994) and 1990 US Census STMP3 Zip Code Files

Note: All coefficients significantly different from zero at the .05 level

Weights to account for sampling probability applied

Having both parents who are foreign-born is positively associated with going to school in a zip code with foreign-born residents (r =.432), yet not so for students in a native household (r = -.451). The ethnic heterogeneity, yet relative density of foreigners, of the areas in which the foreign-born live and send their children to school, may bring results counter to the expectations of social capital theory for immigrants: there may not be strong ethnic ties among foreign families.

Knowing your child's friends' parents has a mildly positive relationship with the child's educational attainment in 1994 and the family's occupational status (r =.359 and .154, respectively), as does sending the child to a school in a zip code with upper-middle class residents (r =.242 and .279, respectively). Parents' educational attainment is also mildly positively associated with these social capital indicators: r =.182 with knowing a child's friends' parents and r =.329 with the index of upper-middle class residents in zip code.

These relationships suggest that social capital may have a role in determining the occupational status of parents and the educational attainment of their children. Social capital, however, does not explain completely the occupational status of a family or the educational attainment of the child. In fact, not one indicator has an effect above 0.5 on a family's occupational status or the child's post-secondary education choices, suggesting that these factors may interact to affect the family's occupational status or the child's schooling success.

One such interaction effect I explore in Chapter Three is the family's immigration status. Table C.2 shows correlation matrices for these same variables by the family's immigration status. Some relationships are similar across each family type. Parents' educational attainment has a strong positive association with family's occupational status (r =.542 for native families, r =.610 for combined families, and r =.657 for immigrant families); and, parents' educational attainment has a relatively strong positive association with child's educational attainment (r =.399 for native families, r =.399 for combined families, and r =.400 for immigrant families).

However, some differences among the sub-populations emerge. Most notable is that the association between the index of upper-middle class residents in a zip code and the percent of residents of the same race or ethnicity as the respondents differ by immigration status. For native and combined families, the index of upper-middle class residents is barely associated with the percentage of co-ethnics in a zip code (r =.049 and r =.055, respectively). For immigrant families, however, there is a negative association (r = -.301). A similar scenario occurs for percent foreign in a zip code (r = .239 for native families, r = .117 for combined families, and r = -.326 for immigrant families).

Table C.2: Pairwise Correlations of Dependent Variables by Family's Immigration Status

Both Parents are Native-born

N = 8,220	1	2	3	4	5	6	7	8	9
1. Education in 1994	1.000								
2. Family occupation	.327	1.000							
3. Parents' education	.399	.542	1.000						
4. % same ethnicity	.076	.059	.087	1.000					
5. % foreign	.021	.082	.067	-.244	1.000				
6. % of recent foreign	.005	.046	.038	-.187	.301	1.000			
7. % same residence	.033	.045	.048	-.008	.141	-.057	1.000		
8. Urban	-.030	.005	.017	-.189	.223	.147	.214	1.000	
9. Know friends	.387	.136	.170	.096	-.058	-.041	-.033	-.083	1.000
10. Index of upper-middle class	.225	.269	.323	.049	.239	.109	.174	.019	.066

One Parent is Foreign-Born

N = 434	1	2	3	4	5	6	7	8	9
1. Education in 1994	1.000								
2. Family occupation	.353	1.000							
3. Parents' education	.399	.610	1.000						
4. % same ethnicity	.038	.070	.030	1.000					
5. % foreign	-.139	-.212	-.274	.035	1.000				
6. % of recent foreign	-.049	-.023	-.010	-.054	.411	1.000			
7. % same residence	-.007	.015	-.086	.130	.199	-.103	1.000		
8. Urban	-.114	-.066	-.104	-.019	.264	.065	.173	1.000	
9. Know friends	.227	.192	.212	.080	-.158	-.038	-.087	-.197	1.000
10. Index of upper-middle class	.319	.370	.409	.055	.117	.103	.143	-.067	.102

(continued on next page)

Table C.2: (continued):

Both Parents are Foreign-born

N = 943	1	2	3	4	5	6	7	8	9
1. Education in 1994	1.000								
2. Family occupation	.379	1.000							
3. Parents' education	.400	.657	1.000						
4. % same ethnicity	-.230	-.212	-.316	1.000					
5. % foreign	-.209	-.232	-.298	.322	1.000				
6. % of recent foreign	-.160	-.183	-.217	-.012	.377	1.000			
7. % same residence	-.010	-.049	-.055	.058	.180	-.139	1.000		
8. Urban	-.123	-.115	-.114	.055	.268	.024	.187	1.000	
9. Know friends	.235	.170	.196	-.118	-.121	-.070	-.071	-.125	1.000
10. Index of upper-middle class	.320	.375	.428	-.301	-.326	-.165	.148	.267	.114

Sources: Student and Parent Files of the National Education Longitudinal Study (1988-1994) and 1990 US Census STMP3 Zip Code Files

Note: All coefficients significantly different from zero at the .05 level

Weights to account for sampling probability applied

These differences further suggest that ethnically homogenous communities or communities with a high percentage of foreigners tend to have less available role models for immigrant families.

Appendix D

Table D.1: Ordinary Least Square Regression Analysis of Effects of Community Context on Occupational Status of Families

Dependent variable = Family occupational status (29.44-63.84)

Reference group = white child with two native-born parents

	Model 1	Model 2	Model 3	Model 4
R²	0.351	0.359	0.369	0.370
Constant	6.910	0.238	-4.953	-5.268
	(3.880)	(4.006)	(3.905)	(3.847)
Parents' Characteristics				
Both parents are foreign-born	11.128	19.019	31.027±	30.316±
	(8.463)	(9.816)	(11.378)	(11.403)
One parent is foreign-born	36.310	43.012	41.470	40.976
	(22.398)	(23.806)	(22.248)	(22.419)
Parents' educational attainment	2.138*	2.116*	1.997*	2.000*
	(0.045)	(0.044)	(0.048)	(0.048)
(Education * both parents	-0.802*	-1.074*	-0.984*	-0.975*
foreign-born)	(0.137)	(0.154)	(0.151)	(0.151)
(Education * one parent	-0.087	-0.247	-0.187	-0.192
foreign-born)	(0.185)	(0.215)	(0.217)	(0.212)
Country mean education	0.970±	1.059±	1.473*	1.553*
	(0.323)	(0.365)	(0.356)	(0.349)
(Country mean * both parents	0.089	-1.483	-2.901[1]	-2.837[1]
foreign-born)	(0.968)	(1.138)	(1.157)	(1.162)
(Country mean * one parent	-3.427	-4.373	-5.196[1]	-5.097[1]
foreign-born	(2.440)	(2.404)	(2.164)	(2.190)
Family arrived in country within		-7.492	-6.470	-6.936
last five years		(8.069)	(7.423)	(7.511)
(Recently arrived * both parents		6.964	5.566	6.057
foreign-born)		(8.226)	(7.605)	(7.689)
(Recently arrived * one parent		3.774	2.414	3.052
foreign-born)		(8.395)	(7.825)	(7.905)
Parents' age		0.130*	0.118*	0.120*
		(0.021)	(0.021)	(0.021)
(Parents' age * both parents		0.052	0.041	0.038
foreign-born)		(0.075)	(0.076)	(0.074)

(continued on next page)

Table D.1: (continued)

	Model 1	Model 2	Model 3	Model 4
(Parents' age * one parent		-0.023	-0.034	-0.043
foreign-born)		(0.153)	(0.153)	(0.154)
Parents' English		0.061	0.059	-0.035
		(0.455)	(0.464)	(0.462)
(Parent's English * both parents		2.127±	2.087±	2.095±
foreign-born)		(0.649)	(0.660)	(0.665)
(Parents' English * one parent		1.203	1.042	1.050
foreign-born)		(0.733)	(0.807)	(0.815)
Segmented Assimilation				
% Same Ethnicity			0.0004	-0.002
			(0.008)	(0.008)
(Same race * both parents			0.050	0.053
foreign-born)			(0.028)	(0.028)
(Same race * one parent			0.028	0.031
foreign-born)			(0.029)	(0.029)
% Foreign			0.056^{+}	0.058^{+}
			(0.025)	(0.024)
(Foreign * both parents			-0.021	-0.017
foreign-born)			(0.046)	(0.045)
(Foreign * one parent			-0.134^{+}	-0.136^{+}
foreign-born)			(0.062)	(0.060)
% Recent Foreigners			0.020	0.010
			(0.008)	(0.008)
(Recent foreigners * both parents			0.008	0.002
foreign-born)			(0.038)	(0.039)
(Recent foreigners * one parent			0.043	0.044
foreign-born)			(0.044)	(0.044)
% Same residence			0.012	0.010
			(0.014)	(0.013)
(Same residence * both parents			-0.040	-0.035
foreign-born			(0.066)	(0.066)
(Same residence * one parent			0.104	0.102
foreign-born)			(0.057)	(0.057)
Urban			0.327	0.301
			(0.434)	(0.430)
(Urban * both parents			0.225	0.201
foreign-born)			(1.285)	(1.281)

(continued on next page)

Table D.1: (continued)

	Model 1	Model 2	Model 3	Model 4
(Urban * one parent			-0.853	-0.572
foreign-born)			(1.400)	(1.395)
Rural			-0.387	-0.374
			(0.450)	(0.449)
(Rural * both parents			0.519	0.669
foreign-born)			(2.160)	(2.149)
(Rural * one parent foreign-born)			1.364	1.274
			(1.928)	(1.931)
Social Capital				
Parents know child's			1.290*	1.280*
friends' parents			(0.311)	(0.309)
(Parents know many * both			-1.569	-1.701
parents foreign-born)			(1.066)	(1.075)
(Parents know many * one			-0.718	-0.608
parent foreign-born)			(1.212)	(1.197)
Index of upper-middle class			0.668*	0.743*
			(0.179)	(0.205)
(Upper-middle class * both			0.719	0.351
parents foreign-born)			(0.610)	(0.653)
(Upper-middle class * one			0.029	-0.153
parent foreign-born)			(0.824)	(0.856)
Ethnic Capital				
Black* index of				-1.006[1]
upper-middle class				(0.494)
Mexican * index				0.413
of upper-middle class				(0.558)
Puerto Rican * index of				2.554[1]
upper-middle class				(1.106)
Cuban * index of				4.136[1]
upper-middle class				(1.743)
Other Latino* index of				1.202
upper-middle class				(0.841)
Chinese * index of				-0.846
upper-middle class				(1.268)
Filipino * index of				1.811
upper-middle class				(1.575)
Korean * index of				-0.573
upper-middle class				(1.203)

(continued on next page)

Table D.1: (continued)

	Model 1	Model 2	Model 3	Model 4
Japanese * index of				0.243
upper-middle class				(1.249)
South East Asian * index of				-1.252
upper-middle class				(1.002)
South Asian * index of				-1.090
upper-middle class				(1.426)
Pacific Islander * index of				-3.289
upper-middle class				(3.213)
Child's Characteristics				
Black	-3.102*	-3.015*	-3.160*	- 3.481*
	(0.502)	(0.514)	(0.607)	(0.617)
(Black * both parents	14.991±	5.678	1.543	2.584
foreign-born	(5.370)	(5.956)	(5.731)	(5.821)
(Black * one parent foreign-born	-16.273	-20.734	-20.415	-19.009
	(13.518)	(13.223)	(12.372)	(12.483)
Mexican	-0.907	-0.749	-1.060	-1.049
	(0.640)	(0.778)	(0.902)	(0.910)
(Mexican* both parents	1.903	1.506	1.184	1.230
foreign-born)	(2.352)	(2.573)	(2.414)	(2.438)
(Mexican * one parent	-8.135	-0.131	-7.004	-6.626
foreign-born	(6.195)	(5.995)	(5.765)	(5.806)
Puerto Rican	-3.553	-3.413	-4.122	-4.484[+]
	(2.244)	(2.120)	(2.390)	(2.095)
(Puerto Rican * both parents	4.115	2.640	5.111	5.275
foreign-born	(3.770)	(3.754)	(4.130)	(3.777)
(Puerto Rican * one parent	-1.977	-2.592	0.534	1.403
foreign-born	(5.998)	(6.077)	(6.358)	(6.410)
Cuban	-4.108	-3.714	-4.057	-3.073
	(3.260)	(3.070)	(2.898)	(2.139)
(Cuban * both parents	5.661	5.325	4.959	2.818
foreign-born	(5.273)	(4.909)	(4.860)	(4.420)
(Cuban * one parent	-0.091	-1.529	1.011	-3.037
foreign-born	(6.269)	(6.011)	(6.046)	(6.017)
Other Latino	0.529	0.688	0.793	0.781
	(0.967)	(0.995)	(1.236)	(1.246)
(Other Latino * both parents	1.593	-0.950	-1.062	-1.002
foreign-born	(3.274)	(3.572)	(3.167)	(3.151)

(continued on next page)

Table D.1: (continued)

	Model 1	Model 2	Model 3	Model 4
(Other Latino * one parent	-12.278	-13.683	-12.862	-13.382
foreign-born	(8.513)	(8.059)	(7.758)	(7.844)
Chinese	-0.263	-0.502	-1.165	-0.480
	(2.146)	(2.034)	(1.993)	(2.107)
(Chinese * both parents	6.582	7.380[+]	9.879±	9.938±
foreign-born	(3.857)	(3.505)	(3.495)	(3.314)
(Chinese * one parent	-0.366	1.020	3.722	4.576
foreign-born	(4.417)	(4.302)	(4.818)	(4.910)
Filipino	-1.879	-1.528	-1.579	-2.143
	(3.005)	(3.035)	(3.029)	(2.950)
(Filipino * both parents	5.770	3.968	6.355	6.486
foreign-born)	(3.752)	(3.786)	(3.917)	(3.805)
(Filipino * one parent	-5.806	-6.198	-3.081	-1.983
foreign-born	(5.145)	(5.074)	(5.280)	(5.278)
Korean	2.562	2.557	3.187	3.232
	(2.229)	(2.221)	(2.208)	(2.255)
(Korean * both parents	-0.916	2.503	6.927	7.344
foreign-born	(3.725)	(3.835)	(4.530)	(4.690)
(Korean * one parent	-5.329	-3.205	0.117	-0.282
foreign-born	(4.733)	(4.618)	(5.428)	(5.510)
Japanese	4.953*	4.871*	3.754±	3.210
	(1.079)	(1.196)	(1.454)	(2.068)
(Japanese * both parents	-5.761	-3.858	1.474	1.801
foreign-born	(3.683)	(4.151)	(4.594)	(4.531)
(Japanese * one parent	-11.840±	-10.602[+]	-7.035	-6.725
foreign-born	(4.430)	(4.715)	(4.914)	(5.318)
South East Asian	-2.540	-2.659	-2.731	-1.943
	(2.833)	(2.790)	(3.144)	(2.711)
(South East Asian * both parents	7.860	2.475	0.996	0.913
foreign-born	(5.799)	(6.484)	(6.228)	(6.012)
(South East Asian * one parent	-15.671	-19.639	-19.192	-18.327
foreign-born	(14.449)	(14.093)	(13.140)	(13.134)
South Asian	-5.106	-4.768	-3.289	-3.359
	(3.672)	(3.541)	(3.454)	(3.345)
(South Asian * both parents	19.075±	12.208	9.246	11.763
foreign-born	(5.886)	(6.256)	(5.895)	(6.008)

(continued on next page)

Table D.1: (continued)

	Model 1	Model 2	Model 3	Model 4
(South Asian * one parent foreign-born	dropped[a]	dropped[a]	dropped[a]	dropped[a]
Pacific Islander	-0.505	-0.400	0.211	-0.920
	(2.059)	(2.017)	(2.144)	(2.478)
(Pacific Islander * both parents foreign-born	2.011	-4.656	-5.058	-2.514
	(5.440)	(5.808)	(5.558)	(5.792)
(Pacific Islander * one parent foreign-born	-8.096	-10.589	-9.454	-9.431
	(10.009)	(9.697)	(9.154)	(9.147)

Sources: National Education Longitudinal Study (1988-1994), International Educational Attainment Data (2000), and STMP3 Zip Code Files from the 1990 U.S. Census

Notes: Huber/white standard errors in parentheses

Weights to account for sampling probability applied

[+]p<.05, ±p<.01, *p<.001

[a] dropped because of insufficient sample size

Appendix E

Table E.1: Ordered Logistic Regression Analysis of Effects of Community Context and Immigration Status on Child's Educational Attainment

Dependent Variable = Post-secondary education in 1994

Reference group = white child with two native-born parents

	Model 1	Model 2	Model 3	Model 4
cut point 1	3.387±	4.972*	5.804*	5.835*
	(1.041)	(1.157)	(1.241)	(1.268)
cut point 2	4.719*	6.396*	7.286*	7.320*
	(1.045)	(1.156)	(1.241)	(1.270)
cut point 3	6.321*	8.106*	9.034*	9.072*
	(1.048)	(1.156)	(1.242)	(1.270)
Parents' Characteristics				
Both parents are foreign-born	3.612	6.976±	6.788±	6.586[1]
	(2.162)	(2.355)	(2.531)	(2.576)
One parent is foreign-born	-2.630	-2.550	-0.398	-4.076
	(2.401)	(2.881)	(3.546)	(3.489)
Parents' educational attainment	0.242*	0.213*	0.165*	0.166*
	(0.015)	(0.015)	(0.016)	(0.015)
(Education * both parents	-0.165*	-0.146*	-0.144*	-0.154*
foreign-born)	(0.028)	(0.030)	(0.036)	(0.036)
(Education * one parent	-0.012	-0.022	-0.021	-0.015
foreign-born	(0.046)	(0.050)	(0.053)	(0.051)
Country mean years of education	0.066	0.093	0.098	0.113
	(0.085)	(0.096)	(0.105)	(0.106)
(Country mean * both parents	-0.035	-0.0212	-0.085	-0.058
foreign-born	(0.235)	(0.269)	(0.283)	(0.293)
(Country mean * one parent	0.430	0.468	0.894[1]	0.906[1]
foreign-born	(0.273)	(0.305)	(0.377)	(0.370)
Parents' English			-0.069	-0.089
			(0.104)	(0.105)
(Parents' English * both parents			0.261	0.265[1]
foreign-born)			(0.135)	(0.134)

(continued on next page)

163

Table E.1: (continued)

	Model 1	Model 2	Model 3	Model 4
(Parents' English * one parent			-0.255	-0.258
foreign-born			(0.003)	(0.212)
Arrived within last five years			-1.842[+]	-1.831[+]
			(0.866)	(0.924)
(Parent recently arrived * both			2.034[+]	2.052[+]
parents foreign-born)			(0.999)	(1.039)
(Parent recently arrived * one			1.154	1.125
parent foreign-born)			(0.985)	(1.027)
Parents' age			0.017±	0.017±
			(0.006)	(0.006)
(Parents' age * both parents			-0.006	-0.008
foreign-born)			(0.016)	(0.015)
(Parents' age * one parent			-0.032	-0.035
foreign-born			(0.021)	(0.020)
Family's occupational status			0.024*	0.024*
			(0.003)	(0.003)
(Occupation * both parents			-0.000	0.002
foreign-born			(0.010)	(0.010)
(Occupation * one parent			0.015	0.015
foreign-born			(0.012)	(0.012)

Segmented Assimilation

	Model 1	Model 2	Model 3	Model 4
% Same Ethnicity		0.001	0.001	0.001
		(0.002)	(0.0020	(0.002)
(Same race * both parents		-0.008	-0.010	-0.009
foreign-born		(0.004)	(0.006)	(0.006)
(Same race * one parent		0.003	-0.000	0.000
foreign-born		(0.006)	(0.005)	(0.005)
% Foreign		0.006	0.005	0.005
		(0.005)	(0.006)	(0.006)
(Foreign * both parents		0.002	0.003	0.001
foreign-born		(0.009)	(0.010)	(0.010)
(Foreign * one parent		-0.019	-0.018	-0.019
foreign-born		(0.014)	(0.013)	(0.013)
% Recent foreigners		0.000	0.000	-0.000
		(0.001)	(0.001)	(0.001)

(continued on next page)

Table E.1: (continued)

	Model 1	Model 2	Model 3	Model 4
(Recent foreigners * both parents		-0.026'	-0.025±	-0.024'
foreign-born		(0.008)	(0.009)	(0.009)
(Recent foreigners * one parent		0.001	-0.002	-0.001
foreign-born		(0.010)	(0.010)	(0.009)
% Same residence		0.009±	0.008±	0.008±
		(0.003)	(0.003)	(0.003)
(Same residence * both parents		-0.019	-0.017	-0.016
foreign-born		(0.001)	(0.012)	(0.012)
(Same residence * one parent		-0.00	-0.003	-0.003
foreign-born		(0.012)	(0.012)	(0.012)
Urban		0.068	0.069	0.065
		(0.115)	(0.116)	(0.117)
(Urban * both parents		-0.266	-0.267	-0.242
foreign-born		(0.221)	(0.231)	(0.232)
(Urban * one parent foreign-born		-0.108	-0.048	0.014
		(0.345)	(0.306)	(0.302)
Rural		0.229±	0.306±	0.310±
		(0.105)	(0.104)	(0.105)
(Rural * both parents foreign-born		-0.659	-0.752	-0.711
		(0.399)	(0.411)	(0.421)
(Rural * one parent foreign-born		0.504	0.489	0.467
		(0.419)	(0.430)	(0.433)
Social Capital				
Parents know many or some of		1.426*	1.423*	1.425*
Child's friends' parents		(0.079)	(0.078)	(0.077)
(Parents know many * both parents		-0.897*	-0.941*	-0.910*
foreign-born		(0.202)	(0.202)	(0.206)
(parents know many * one parent		-0.807*	-0.739±	-0.721±
foreign-born		(0.261)	(0.252)	(0.248)
Index of upper-middle class		0.275*	0.244*	0.263*
		(0.057)	(0.056)	(0.059)
(Upper-middle class * both parents		-0.091	-0.941*	-0.214
foreign-born)		(0.112)	(0.202)	(0.131)
(Upper-middle class * one parent		0.098	0.154	0.116
foreign-born		(0.135)	(0.124)	(0.123)

(continued on next page)

Table E.1: (continued)

	Model 1	Model 2	Model 3	Model 4
Ethnic Capital				
Black* index of upper-middle class				-0.236
				(0.243)
Mexican * index of upper-middle class				0.066
				(0.147)
Puerto Rican * index of upper-middle class				0.880[+]
				(0.348)
Cuban * index of upper-middle class				0.375
				(0.233)
Other Latino* index of upper-middle class				-0.319[+]
				(0.155)
Chinese * index of upper-middle class				-0.287
				(0.298)
Filipino * index of upper-middle class				0.000
				(0.175)
Korean * index of upper-middle class				0.349
				(0.373)
Japanese * index of upper-middle class				0.134
				(0.326)
South East Asian * index of upper-middle class				0.767±
				(0.274)
South Asian * index of upper-middle class				0.205
				(0.390)
Pacific Islander * index of upper-middle class residents				1.316[+]
				(0.621)
Child's Characteristics				
Black	-0.338[+]	-0.036	0.045	-0.041
	(0.133)	(0.210)	(0.216)	(0.286)
(Black * both parents foreign-born	0.491	0.394	-0.201	0.109
	(1.313)	(1.275)	(1.306)	(1.336)
(Black * one parent foreign-born	2.253	3.013	5.380[+]	5.647[+]
	(1.559)	(1.880)	(2.278)	(2.244)
Mexican	-0.218	0.020	0.031	0.016
	(0.168)	(0.207)	(0.228)	(0.245)
(Mexican * both parents foreign-born	-0.769	-0.877	-0.813	-0.762
	(0.556)	(0.521)	(0.523)	(0.529)

(continued on next page)

Table E.1: (continued)

	Model 1	Model 2	Model 3	Model 4
(Mexican * one parent	1.113	1.697[i]	2.408[i]	2.479±
foreign-born	(0.746)	(0.826)	(0.967)	(0.955)
Puerto Rican	-0.769	-0.599	-0.539	-0.617
	(0.472)	(0.581)	(0.552)	(0.489)
(Puerto Rican * both parents	-0.809	-1.439	-1.621	-1.581[i]
foreign-born	(0.799)	(0.879)	(0.846)	(0.789)
(Puerto Rican * one parent	0.604	1.405	1.643	1.787
foreign-born	(0.812)	(1.099)	(1.083)	(1.071)
Cuban	-0.159	0.018	0.201	0.253
	(0.276)	(0.347)	(0.351)	(0.399)
(Cuban * both parents	-0.817	-1.338[i]	-1.439[i]	-1.495[i]
foreign-born	(0.582)	(0.649)	(0.684)	(0.731)
(Cuban * one parent foreign-born	0.029	0.611	0.691	0.386
	(0.854)	(1.127)	(1.168)	(1.212)
Other Latino	-0.304	-0.047	-0.086	-0.188
	(0.196)	(0.282)	(0.289)	(0.311)
(Other Latino * both parents	0.489	0.232	0.166	0.443
foreign-born)	(0.798)	(0.768)	(0.803)	(0.789)
(Other Latino * one parent	2.340[i]	2.728[i]	4.093±	4.527±
foreign-born	(0.649)	(1.210)	(1.368)	(1.347)
Chinese	0.657	0.921	0.961	1.151
	(0.649)	(0.777)	(0.781)	(0.733)
(Chinese * both parents	1.261	0.757	0.555	0.671
foreign-born	(0.938)	(1.088)	(1.041)	(1.009)
(Chinese * one parent	1.384	1.621	1.342	1.558
foreign-born	(1.179)	(1.343)	(1.222)	(1.205)
Filipino	0.618	0.780	0.870	0.829
	(0.365)	(0.477)	(0.491)	(0.511)
(Filipino * both parents	0.618	-1.285[i]	-1.671[i]	-1.542[i]
foreign-born)	(0.365)	(0.653)	(0.688)	(0.698)
(Filipino * one parent	0.194	0.813	1.111	1.165
foreign-born	(0.633)	(0.927)	(0.941)	(0.940)
Korean	0.975	1.429	1.396	1.222
	(0.760)	(0.891)	(0.903)	(0.891)
(Korean * both parents	-0.167	-1.308	-1.291	-1.430
foreign-born	(0.921)	(1.232)	(1.263)	(1.259)

(continued on next page)

Table E.1: (continued)

	Model 1	Model 2	Model 3	Model 4
(Korean * one parent	-0.758	-0.675	-1.535	-1.413
foreign- born)	(0.990)	(1.244)	(1.246)	(1.237)
Japanese	0.375	0.286	0.179	-0.024
	(0.375)	(0.455)	(0.470)	(0.590)
(Japanese * both parents	-0.855	-1.638	-1.567	-1.501
foreign-born	(0.697)	(1.090)	(1.138)	(1.165)
(Japanese * one parent	-1.262	-0.595	-0.879	-0.775
foreign-born	(0.927)	(1.007)	(0.935)	(1.009)
South East Asian	0.893	0.640	0.719	0.383
	(0.934)	(0.875)	(1.050)	(0.650)
(South East Asian * both parents	-0.146	0.137	-0.225	0.412
foreign-born	(1.551)	(1.453)	(1.593)	(1.400)
(South East Asian * one parent	0.979	2.234	4.272	4.317
foreign-born	(2.055)	(2.205)	(2.606)	(2.460)
South Asian	-0.141	0.623	0.738	0.748
	(0.864)	(1.052)	(0.916)	(0.908)
(South Asian * both parents	1.474	0.300	-0.345	-0.347
foreign-born	(1.422)	(1.503)	(1.435)	(1.514)
(South Asian* one parent	dropped[a]	dropped[a]	dropped[a]	dropped[a]
foreign-born				
Pacific Islander	-0.649	-0.086	-0.116	0.278
	(0.354)	(0.383)	(0.426)	(0.413)
(Pacific Islander * both parents	-0.144	-0.877	-1.358	-1.955
foreign-born	(0.987)	(0.961)	(1.029)	(1.039)
(Pacific Islander * one parent	3.267	3.803	4.919[+]	5.311[+]
foreign-born	(1.941)	(2.343)	(2.345)	(2.243)
Child arrived in U.S.	-0.506	-0.376	-0.394	-0.397
within last five years	(0.739)	(0.733)	(0.844)	(0.819)
(Child recently arrived * both	-0.141	-0.266	-0.204	-0.206
parents foreign-born	(0.809)	(0.822)	(0.964)	(0.931)
(Child recently arrive * one parent	1.461	1.886	2.276	2.209
foreign-born	(0.996)	(1.055)	(1.198)	(1.151)
Grade when child started	-0.124[+]	-0.085	-0.054	-0.066
school in the U.S.	(0.062)	(0.055)	(0.053)	(0.056)
(Grade child started * both parents	0.242±	0.229±	-0.054	0.190*
foreign-born	(0.086)	(0.085)	(0.053)	(0.089)

(continued on next page)

Table E.1: (continued)

	Model 1	Model 2	Model 3	Model 4
(Grade child started * one parent	-0.106	-0.150	-0.182	-0.176
foreign-born	(0.129)	(0.120)	(0.123)	(0.128)
Child is Limited English Proficient	-0.012	0.035	-0.016	-0.016
	(0.095)	(0.094)	(0.102)	(0.102)
(LEP * both parents foreign-born	-0.012	0.298	0.547	0.498
	(0.095)	(0.283)	(0.286)	(0.292)
(LEP * one parent foreign-born	-0.227	-0.253	-0.393	-0.376
	(0.236)	(0.268)	(0.269)	(0.268)
Female child	0.259*	0.175±	0.189±	0.191±
	(0.061)	(0.063)	(0.063)	(0.063)
(Female * both parents	-0.392^{1}	-0.372^{1}	-0.358^{1}	-0.348
foreign-born	(0.176)	(0.179)	(0.178)	(0.178)
(Female * one parent	0.363	0.229	0.130	0.167
foreign-born	(0.258)	(0.239)	(0.240)	(0.237)
Parental involvement	0.602*	0.475*	0.462*	0.464*
	(0.068)	(0.069)	(0.070)	(0.068)
(Involvement * both parents	-0.095	-0.054	-0.107	-0.105
foreign-born	(0.217)	(0.211)	(0.191)	(0.190)
(Involvement * one parent	-0.363	-0.325	-0.269	-0.288
foreign-born	(0.212)	(0.223)	(0.227)	(0.222)
Foreign-born child	-0.159	-0.058	-0.080	-0.164
	(0.208)	(0.217)	(0.191)	(0.183)

$N = 10,547$

Sources: National Education Longitudinal Study (1988-1994), International Educational Attainment Data (2000), and STMP3 Zip Code Files from the 1990 U.S. Census

Notes: Huber/white standard errors in parentheses

Weights to account for sampling probability applied

^{1}p<.05, ±p<.01, *p<.001

^{a} dropped because of insufficient sample size

Appendix F

Table F.1: Parental Involvement Variable Construction

	Question	Scale	Mean	St. Dev.
Parent-Student communication about school				
Child's perception	Since the beginning of the school year, how often have you discussed the following with either or both of your parents or guardians?	0: (not at all)	2.041	0.761
		1.5: (once or twice)		
		3: (three or more times)		
	a. Selecting courses or programs at school			
	b. School activities or events of particular interest to you			
	c. Things you've studied in class			
Parent's perception	Parents differ in how much they talk to their children about what they do in school. How often do you or your spouse/partner talk with your eighth grader about his or her experience in school?	0: (not at all)	2.726	0.509
		1: (rarely)		
		2: (occasionally)		
		3: (regularly)		
Parent Supervision at Home				
Child's perception	How often do you your parents or guardians do the following?	0: (never)	1.953	0.611
	a. Check on whether you have done your homework	1: (rarely)		
	b. Require you to do work or chores around the home	2: (sometimes)		
	c. Limit the amount of time you can spend watching television	3: (often)		
	d. Limit the amount of time for going out with friends on school nights			

(continued on next page)

Table F.1: (continued)

Wave	Question	Scale	Mean	St. Dev.
Parent Supervision at Home (continued)				
Parent's perception	Are there any family rules that are enforced for your eighth grader about any of the following activities?		0.001	0.548
	a. Maintaining a certain grade average			
	b. Doing homework			
	c. Doing household chores			
	Are there any rules for your eighth grader about any of the following television-related activities?	1: (yes) 0: (no)		
	a. What program he or she may watch			
	b. How many hours he or she may watch television			
	c. How many hours he or she may watch television on school days			
	How often do you or your spouse/partner help your eighth grader with his or her homework?	0: (seldom or never) 24: (1 or 2x month) 104: (1 or 2x week) 365: (almost every day)		

(continued on next page)

Table F.1: (continued)

Wave	Question	Scale	Mean	St. Dev.
Parent Involvement in School-related Activities				
Child's Perception	Since the beginning of the school year, has either of your parents or guardians done any of the following?	0: (did not participate in any of the four)	1.915	1.097
		1: (participated in one)		
	a. Attended a school meeting	2: (participated in two)		
	b. Phoned or spoken to your teacher or counselor	3: (participated in three)		
	c. Visited your class	4: (participated in all)		
	d. Attended a school event such as a play, concert, gym exhibit, sports competition, honor ceremony, or science fair where you participated?			
Parent's perception	Since your eighth graders' school opened last fall, how many times have you or your spouse/ partner contacted the school about each of the following?	0: (none)	0.001	0.56
		1.5: (once or twice)		
	a. Your eighth grader's academic performance	3.5 (three or four times)		
	b. Your eighth grader's academic program for the year	5: (more than four times)		
	c. Your eighth grader's behavior in school			
	d. Participating in school fund raising activities			
	e. Providing information for school records such as your address or work telephone number			
	f. Doing volunteer work such as supervising lunch, or chaperoning a field trip			
	Do you or your spouse/ partner do any of the following at your eighth grader's school?	0: (no)		
	a. Belong to a parent-teacher organization?	1: (yes)		
	b. Attend meetings of parent-teacher organization			
	c. Take part in the activities of a parent-teacher organization			
	d. Act as a volunteer at the school			

Source: Student and Parent Files of the National Educational Longitudinal Study (1988)

Appendix G

Table G.1: Ordered Logistic Regression Analyses of the Effects of Parental Involvement on Post-Secondary Schooling

Dependent variable= Student's Post-Secondary Education Schooling in 1994

	Model 1	Model 2	Model 3	Model 4	Model 5	Model 6	Model 7	Model 8
cut point 1	3.274*	3.201*	3.336*	3.173*	3.265*	3.290*	3.259*	3.072*
	(0.602)	(0.605)	(0.654)	(0.644)	(0.600)	(0.605)	(0.593)	(0.655)
cut point 2	4.718*	4.647*	4.780*	4.617*	4.712*	4.734*	4.705*	4.521*
	(0.609)	(0.612)	(0.66)	(0.652)	(0.609)	(0.612)	(0.600)	(0.664)
cut point 3	6.425*	6.354*	6.487*	6.324*	6.422*	6.441*	6.412*	6.231*
	(0.618)	(0.621)	(0.670)	(0.662)	(0.618)	(0.622)	(0.609)	(0.674)
Both parents foreign-born	2.752+	2.598+	3.345+	2.727+	2.749+	2.826+	2.766+	3.320**
	(1.142)	(1.134)	(1.310)	(1.146)	(1.148)	(1.129)	(1.130)	(1.272)
One parent foreign-born	3.165	2.539	2.626	3.188	3.337	3.481	3.467	2.981
	(1.749)	(1.689)	(1.856)	(1.721)	(1.716)	(1.839)	(1.721)	(1.856)
Child's perception of parent-student communication	-0.048							-0.048
	(0.037)							(0.038)
(child: communication * both parents foreign)	0.093							0.124
	(0.124)							(0.131)

(continued on next page)

Table G.1: (continued)

	Model 1	Model 2	Model 3	Model 4	Model 5	Model 6	Model 7	Model 8
(child: communication * one parent foreign)		0.276						0.378
		(0.161)						(0.177)
Parent's perception of parent-student communication			0.022					-0.024
			(0.056)					(0.056)
(parent: communication * both parents foreign)			-0.192					-0.195
			(0.157)					(0.176)
(parent: communication * one parent foreign)			0.177					0.108
			(0.329)					(0.413)
Child's perception of parental supervision at home				-0.054				-0.044
				(0.054)				(0.056)
(child: supervision * both parents foreign)				0.015				-0.006
				(0.147)				(0.155)
(child: supervision * one parent foreign)				-0.014				-0.113
				(0.185)				(0.182)
Parent's perception of parental supervision at home					0.154⁻			0.156⁻
					(0.067)			(0.065)
(parent: supervision * both parents foreign)					-0.176			-0.145
					(0.150)			(0.163)

(continued on next page)

Table G.1: (continued)

	Model 1	Model 2	Model 3	Model 4	Model 5	Model 6	Model 7	Model 8
(parent: supervision * one parent foreign)					0.353			0.248
					(0.258)			(0.250)
Child's perception of parental involvement in school						0.009		0.021
						(0.030)		(0.031)
(child: parental involvement * both parents foreign)						-0.048		-0.072
						(0.087)		(0.090)
(child: parental involvement * one parent foreign)						-0.115		-0.150
						(0.118)		(0.126)
Parent's perception of parental involvement in school							0.043	0.020
							(0.072)	(0.069)
(parent: parental involvement * both parents foreign)							0.074	0.139
							(0.184)	(0.190)
(parent: parental involvement * one parent foreign)							0.295	0.235
							(0.223)	(0.250)
Parents' Characteristics								
Parents' years of schooling	0.299*	0.299*	0.299*	0.299*	0.299*	0.299*	0.299*	0.299*
	(0.020)	(0.020)	(0.020)	(0.020)	(0.020)	(0.020)	(0.020)	(0.020)

(continued on next page)

Table G.1: (continued)

	Model 1	Model 2	Model 3	Model 4	Model 5	Model 6	Model 7	Model 8
(Education * both parents foreign-born)	-0.228*	-0.228*	-0.229*	-0.228*	-0.228*	-0.227*	-0.228*	-0.230*
	(0.039)	(0.039)	(0.038)	(0.020)	(0.039)	(0.038)	(0.039)	(0.038)
(Education * one parent foreign-born)	-0.034	-0.030	-0.034	-0.034	-0.054	-0.037	-0.037	-0.055
	(0.057)	(0.058)	(0.057)	(0.057)	(0.055)	(0.056)	(0.057)	(0.055)
Parents' English ability	-0.085	-0.086	-0.085	-0.086	-0.084	-0.085	-0.087	-0.086
	(0.079)	(0.080)	(0.079)	(0.079)	(0.080)	(0.079)	(0.079)	(0.080)
(Parent's English * both parents foreign-born)	0.350±	0.353±	0.349±	0.351±	0.350±	0.349±	0.351±	0.351⁻
	(0.119)	(0.120)	(0.057)	(0.120)	(0.119)	(0.120)	(0.119)	(0.120)
(Parents' English * one parent foreign-born)	-0.087	-0.077	-0.085	-0.090	-0.089	-0.087	-0.127	-0.108
	(0.217)	(0.212)	(0.079)	(0.215)	(0.220)	(0.219)	(0.213)	(0.207)
Parent arrived less than five years ago	-0.424	-0.420	-0.418	-0.408	-0.390	-0.432	-0.434	-0.402
	(0.701)	(0.705)	(0.699)	(0.696)	(0.707)	(0.702)	(0.696)	(0.708)
(Parent recently arrived * both parents foreign-born)	0.093	0.090	0.064	0.078	0.059	0.121	0.088	0.047
	(0.770)	(0.74)	(0.771)	(0.765)	(0.776)	(0.766)	(0.763)	(0.775)
(Parent recently arrived * one parent foreign-born)	0.142	0.154	0.142	0.132	0.207	0.121	0.130	0.182
	(0.891)	(0.904)	(0.886)	(0.888)	(0.876)	(0.889)	(0.884)	(0.897)
Parents' age	0.015⁻	0.015⁻	0.015⁻	0.015⁻	0.015⁻	0.015⁻	0.015⁻	0.015⁻
	(0.006)	(0.006)	(0.006)	(0.006)	(0.006)	(0.006)	(0.006)	(0.006)

(continued on next page)

Table G.1: (continued)

	Model 1	Model 2	Model 3	Model 4	Model 5	Model 6	Model 7	Model 8
(Parents' age * both parents foreign-born)	-0.002	-0.002	-0.003	-0.003	-0.002	-0.003	-0.003	-0.003
	(0.016)	(0.016)	(0.016)	(0.016)	(0.016)	(0.016)	(0.015)	(0.016)
(Parents' age * one parent foreign-born)	-0.036	-0.032	-0.035	-0.035	-0.036	-0.036	-0.037	-0.033
	(0.026)	(0.026)	(0.025)	(0.026)	(0.025)	(0.025)	(0.025)	(0.024)
Students' Characteristics								
Black	-0.113	-0.114	-0.113	-0.115	-0.114	-0.113	-0.119	-0.117
	(0.129)	(0.129)	(0.129)	(0.130)	(0.130)	(0.129)	(0.125)	(0.128)
(Black * both parents foreign-born)	0.453	0.454	0.420	0.461	0.450	0.461	0.421	0.381
	(0.590)	(0.591)	(0.590)	(0.593)	(0.591)	(0.587)	(0.592)	(0.594)
(Black * one parent foreign-born)	-0.270	-0.340	-0.241	-0.250	-0.210	-0.265	-0.224	-0.208
	(0.597)	(0.592)	(0.581)	(0.594)	(0.531)	(0.578)	(0.580)	(0.520)
Mexican	-0.146	-0.147	-0.148	-0.143	-0.137	-0.146	-0.151	-0.134
	(0.160)	(0.160)	(0.150)	(0.160)	(0.161)	(0.160)	(0.160)	(0.161)
(Mexican * both parents foreign-born)	-0.219	-0.212	-0.233	-0.225	-0.230	-0.199	-0.262	-0.281
	(0.381)	(0.380)	(0.382)	(0.380)	(0.382)	(0.381)	(0.373)	(0.373)
(Mexican * one parent foreign-born)	-0.350	-0.250	-0.357	-0.369	-0.356	-0.366	-0.443	-0.341
	(0.474)	(0.439)	(0.472)	(0.472)	(0.476)	(0.472)	(0.483)	(0.444)
Puerto Rican	-1.159[+]	-1.170[+]	-1.155[+]	-1.165±	-1.152±	-1.155[+]	-1.151[+]	-1.161[+]
	(0.453)	(0.459)	(0.452)	(0.453)	(0.447)	(0.453)	(0.452)	(0.453)

(continued on next page)

Table G.1: (continued)

	Model 1	Model 2	Model 3	Model 4	Model 5	Model 6	Model 7	Model 8
(Puerto Rican * both parents foreign-born)	-0.081	-0.071	-0.093	-0.075	-0.093	-0.059	-0.118	-0.097
	(0.716)	(0.722)	(0.715)	(0.716)	(0.716)	(0.726)	(0.715)	(0.724)
(Puerto Rican * one parent foreign-born)	0.168	0.268	0.181	0.182	0.110	0.155	0.074	0.199
	(0.736)	(0.721)	(0.734)	(0.737)	(0.699)	(0.751)	(0.718)	(0.683)
Cuban	-0.248	-0.242	-0.250	-0.246	-0.267	-0.250	-0.251	-0.263
	(0.346)	(0.349)	(0.344)	(0.351)	(0.334)	(0.345)	(0.341)	(0.340)
(Cuban * both parents foreign-born)	-0.137	-0.137	-0.171	-0.138	-0.115	-0.107	-0.167	-0.166
	(0.536)	(0.537)	(0.539)	(0.540)	(0.699)	(0.538)	(0.529)	(0.534)
(Cuban * one parent foreign-born)	-1.057	-1.165	-0.995	-1.026	-0.964	-1.058	-1.190	-1.124
	(0.871)	(0.882)	(0.885)	(0.890)	(0.828)	(0.834)	(0.918)	(0.875)
Other Latino	-0.168	-0.169	-0.168	-0.167	-0.167	-0.167	-0.166	-0.164
	(0.185)	(0.186)	(0.186)	(0.186)	(0.184)	(0.186)	(0.187)	(0.187)
(Other Latino * both parents foreign-born)	1.019⁻	1.038⁻	1.035⁻	1.013⁺	1.021⁻	1.029⁻	0.965	1.003⁻
	(0.435)	(0.435)	(0.437)	(0.433)	(0.434)	(0.434)	(0.443)	(0.442)
(Other Latino * one parent foreign-born)	0.475	0.434	0.509	0.469	0.387	0.549	0.520	0.373
	(0.502)	(0.512)	(0.521)	(0.498)	(0.513)	(0.502)	(0.521)	(0.551)
Chinese	1.396⁻	1.390⁻	1.395⁻	1.391⁻	1.420⁻	1.396	1.402	1.414⁻
	(0.737)	(0.743)	(0.738)	(0.743)	(0.735)	(0.738)	(0.741)	(0.748)

(continued on next page)

Table G.1: (continued)

	Model 1	Model 2	Model 3	Model 4	Model 5	Model 6	Model 7	Model 8
(Chinese* both parents foreign-born)	0.764	0.782	0.752	0.764	0.744	0.780	0.751	0.757
	(0.875)	(0.880)	(0.879)	(0.877)	(0.871)	(0.876)	(0.80)	(0.888)
(Chinese* one parent foreign-born)	-0.688	-0.710	-0.730	-0.688	-0.837	-0.660	-0.681	-0.822
	(1.189)	(1.217)	(1.184)	(1.190)	(1.194)	(1.170)	(1.195)	(1.196)
Filipino	0.292	0.278	0.288	0.307	0.265	0.295	0.283	0.269
	(0.364)	(0.364)	(0.364)	(0.365)	(0.366)	(0.365)	(0.363)	(0.367)
(Filipino * both parents foreign-born)	-0.406	-0.399	-0.413	-0.408	-0.375	-0.391	-0.416	-0.399
	(0.509)	(0.512)	(0.512)	(0.516)	(0.509)	(0.508)	(0.505)	(0.514)
(Filipino * one parent foreign-born)	-0.166	-0.144	-0.175	-0.167	-0.191	-0.149	-0.171	-0.120
	(0.554)	(0.551)	(0.553)	(0.561)	(0.582)	(0.560)	(0.548)	(0.583)
Korean	1.171	1.163	1.166	1.172	1.138	1.173	1.147	1.130
	(0.894)	(0.895)	(0.894)	(0.898)	(0.903)	(0.892)	(0.901)	(0.908)
(Korean * both parents foreign-born)	-0.118	-0.112	-0.135	-0.119	-0.081	-0.107	-0.115	-0.121
	(0.970)	(0.973)	(0.970)	(0.974)	(0.978)	(0.971)	(0.974)	(0.984)
(Korean * one parent foreign-born)	-0.299	-0.200	-0.287	-0.284	-0.162	-0.291	-0.359	-0.056
	(1.029)	(1.030)	(1.042)	(1.041)	(1.050)	(1.021)	(1.050)	(1.072)
Japanese	0.078	0.059	0.075	0.076	0.070	0.078	0.077	0.054
	(0.507)	(0.517)	(0.506)	(0.504)	(0.514)	(0.507)	(0.508)	(0.523)

(continued on next page)

Table G.1: (continued)

	Model 1	Model 2	Model 3	Model 4	Model 5	Model 6	Model 7	Model 8
(Japanese * both parents foreign-born)	-0.591	-0.575	-0.630	-0.587	-0.585	-0.573	-0.574	-0.577
	(0.882)	(0.891)	(0.870)	(0.881)	(0.883)	(0.862)	(0.887)	(0.864)
(Japanese * one parent foreign-born)	-0.716	-0.758	-0.769	-0.755	-0.547	-0.565	-0.669	-0.543
	(0.889)	(0.918)	(0.876)	(0.888)	(0.921)	(0.919)	(0.872)	(0.941)
South East Asian	-1.420	0.276	0.286	0.304	0.272	0.296	0.310	0.302
	(1.291)	(0.756)	(0.770)	(0.768)	(0.781)	(0.771)	(0.766)	(0.767)
(South East Asian * both parents foreign-born)	1.180	0.850	0.786	0.801	0.838	0.826	0.787	0.787
	(0.668)	(0.848)	(0.867)	(0.858)	(0.870)	(0.862)	(0.858)	(0.856)
(South East Asian * one parent foreign-born)	-0.134	-1.443	-1.403	-1.415	-1.391	-1.396	-1.447	-1.378
	(0.796)	(1.298)	(1.293)	(1.295)	(1.292)	(1.258)	(1.280)	(1.264)
South Asian	1.180	1.207	1.186	1.190	1.138	1.176	1.174	1.154
	(0.668)	(0.669)	(0.666)	(0.677)	(0.682)	(0.664)	(0.679)	(0.693)
(South Asian * both parents foreign-born)	-0.134	-0.155	-0.206	-0.144	-0.091	-0.107	-0.151	-0.187
	(0.796)	(0.798)	(0.789)	(0.804)	(0.806)	(0.792)	(0.803)	(0.806)
(South Asian * one parent foreign-born)	dropped[a]	dropped[a]	dropped[a]	dropped[a]	dropped[a]	dropped[a]	dropped[a]	dropped[a]
Pacific Islander	-0.341	-0.331	-0.344	-0.346	-0.372	-0.343	-0.350	-0.372
	(0.301)	(0.303)	(0.302)	(0.299)	(0.305)	(0.300)	(0.304)	(0.305)

(continued on next page)

Table G.1: (continued)

	Model 1	Model 2	Model 3	Model 4	Model 5	Model 6	Model 7	Model 8
(Pacific Islander * both parents foreign-born)	-0.601	-0.615	-0.615	-0.606	-0.575	-0.594	-0.586	-0.596
	(0.599)	(0.599)	(0.613)	(0.597)	(0.605)	(0.598)	(0.591)	(0.601)
(Pacific Islander * one parent foreign-born)	1.512	1.535[+]	1.482	1.537	1.678	1.421	1.641	1.723
	(1.702)	(1.702)	(1.717)	(1.727)	(1.811)	(1.688)	(749)	(1.882)
Urban	0.077	0.072	0.077	0.076	0.080	0.078	0.075	0.074
	(0.108)	(0.107)	(0.108)	(0.108)	(0.108)	(0.107)	(0.106)	(0.106)
(urban * both parents foreign-born)	-0.245	-0.245	-0.240	-0.246	-0.247	-0.248	-0.240	-0.249
	(0.239)	(0.237)	(0.241)	(0.240)	(0.239)	(0.239)	(0.239)	(0.240)
(urban * one parent foreign-born)	-0.020	0.026	-0.045	-0.013	0.027	-0.051	-0.004	0.066
	(0.361)	(0.342)	(0.364)	(0.364)	(0.363)	(0.369)	(0.357)	(0.354)
Rural	0.079	0.077	0.079	0.079	0.080	0.080	0.078	0.078
	(0.071)	(0.070)	(0.070)	(0.071)	(0.070)	(0.070)	(0.070)	(0.069)
(rural * both parents foreign-born)	-0.260	-0.254	-0.254	-0.257	-0.261	-0.262	-0.245	-0.226
	(0.352)	(0.352)	(0.351)	(0.353)	(0.352)	(0.354)	(0.353)	(0.357)
(rural * one parent foreign-born)	0.465	0.482	0.479	0.569	0.489	0.469	0.464	0.534
	(0.326)	(0.325)	(0.324)	(0.326)	(0.320)	(0.329)	(0.328)	(0.324)
Female	0.234*	0.235*	0.234*	0.235*	0.231*	0.234*	0.234*	0.234*
	(0.066)	(0.066)	(0.066)	(0.066)	(0.066)	(0.067)	(0.066)	(0.066)

(continued on next page)

Table G.1: (continued)

	Model 1	Model 2	Model 3	Model 4	Model 5	Model 6	Model 7	Model 8
(Female * both parents foreign-born)	-0.350	-0.350	-0.350	-0.352	-0.347	-0.350	-0.336	-0.333
	(0.194)	(0.194)	(0.194)	(0.194)	(0.194)	(0.194)	(0.193)	(0.195)
(Female * one parent foreign-born)	0.259	0.209	0.291	0.265	0.266	0.250	0.266	0.216
	(0.255)	(0.253)	(0.254)	(0.249)	(0.252)	(0.253)	(0.246)	(0.239)
Student is Limited English Proficient	-0.060	-0.059	-0.060	-0.062	-0.063	-0.060	-0.061	-0.064
	(0.105)	(0.105)	(0.105)	(0.105)	(0.106)	(0.105)	(0.105)	(0.105)
(LEP * both parents foreign-born)	0.653⁺	0.655⁺	0.654⁺	0.653⁺	0.658⁺	0.649⁺	0.670⁺	0.677
	(0.314)	(0.315)	(0.313)	(0.314)	(0.315)	(0.314)	(0.305)	(0.304)
(LEP * one parent foreign-born)	-0.214	-0.264	-0.201	-0.203	-0.212	-0.219	-0.222	-0.272
	(0.304)	(0.305)	(0.291)	(0.306)	(0.301)	(0.303)	(0.303)	(0.295)
Grade student started school in the U.S.	-0.079	-0.079	-0.079	-0.080	-0.081	-0.079	-0.081	-0.083
	(0.057)	(0.057)	(0.058)	(0.058)	(0.058)	(0.058)	(0.058)	(0.059)
(Grade child started * both parents foreign-born)	0.169	0.171	0.167	0.169	0.171	0.165	0.175	0.172
	(0.091)	(0.091)	(0.092)	(0.090)	(0.091)	(0.090)	(0.090)	(0.090)
(Grade child started * one parent foreign-born)	-0.130	-0.140	-0.136	-0.132	-0.137	-0.133	-0.135	-0.182
	(0.119)	(0.123)	(0.118)	(0.119)	(0.115)	(0.116)	(0.117)	(0.117)
Social Capital								
Parents know child's friends' parents	1.501*	1.500*	1.501*	1.502*	1.507*	1.501*	1.502*	1.508*
	(0.075)	(0.075)	(0.075)	(0.075)	(0.074)	(0.075)	(0.074)	(0.074)

(continued on next page)

Table G.1: (continued)

	Model 1	Model 2	Model 3	Model 4	Model 5	Model 6	Model 7	Model 8
(parents know many * both parents foreign-born)	-0.924*	-0.919*	-0.921*	-0.930*	-0.933*	-0.937*	-0.922*	-0.933*
	(0.209)	(0.210)	(0.209)	(0.279)	(0.207)	(0.216)	(0.210)	(0.215)
(parents know many * one parent foreign-born)	-0.958±	-0.971*	-0.951±	-0.959±	-0.888±	-0.978±	-0.969*	-0.942±
	(0.278)	(0.273)	(0.276)	(0.279)	(0.276)	(0.285)	(0.273)	(0.272)
Index of upper-middle class in zip code	0.225±	0.224*	0.225*	0.225*	0.227*	0.225*	0.223*	0.226*
	(0.044)	(0.044)	(0.044)	(0.044)	(0.044)	(0.044)	(0.044)	(0.044)
(upper-middle class * both parents foreign-born)	-0.028	-0.031	-0.023	-0.027	-0.029	-0.027	-0.025	-0.026
	(0.104)	(0.104)	(0.104)	(0.104)	(0.104)	(0.104)	(0.103)	(0.103)
(upper-middle class * one parent foreign-born)	-0.028	0.101	0.107	0.098	0.132	0.100	0.093	0.171
	(0.104)	(0.164)	(0.146)	(0.159)	(0.164)	(0.155)	(0.164)	(0.147)

N= 10,547

Sources: Student, Parent, and Teacher Files of the National Education Longitudinal Study (1988-1994) and 1990 U.S. Census (STMP3 zip code files)

Notes: Huber White/Sandwich standard errors in parentheses

Weights to account for probability of being sampled employed

+ p<.05, ± p<.01, * p<.001

[a] Dropped because of insufficient sample size

Notes

CHAPTER 1

[1] "First-generation" refers to people who were born in a different country and now reside in the United States. "Second-generation" refers to their children: native-born people of immigrant parents. Rumbaut (2004) elaborates further on the distinctions within generations: 1.75 generation refers to children who arrived before school-age (age 0-5); 1.5 generation refers to children in middle childhood (age 6-12); 1.25 generation refers to children who arrived in their teens and adolescence (age 13-17). 2.5 generation refers to the children of one foreign-born parent and one native-born parent. The 2.5 generation is a focal point of the research in Chapters 4 and 5 and will be discussed further.

[2] The official poverty line is defined by the Office of Management and Budget based on the most recent data available from the Bureau of the Census. The definition is based on a set of money income thresholds that varies by family size and composition, and does not take into account non-cash benefits or taxes. States are allowed to determine their own poverty lines-but should not exceed 125% of the federal poverty line. In 2003, 35.9 million people lived below the poverty line (DeNavas-Walt, et al. 2004).

[3]   Hirschman (2001) includes residence in a central city area as part of his test
      of segmented assimilation, but falls short of exploring the concentration of
      immigrants or co-ethnic peers within that metropolitan area.

CHAPTER 2

[1]   Subsequent chapters use data from the 1988-1994 waves of the National
      Education Longitudinal Study, which follows eighth grader students from
      1988 through out their school career and beyond. Because the students in
      this data set are in school around 1990, I use the 1990 wave of the U.S.
      Census in this and subsequent chapters to make the adult (or, parents')
      occupation and education information comparable. Age 28-55 is the same
      age range as the parents of eighth graders in the National Education
      Longitudinal Study sample that I use in analyses in the subsequent
      chapters.

[2]   Hendricks (2001:418-419) proposes a theory to explain why immigrants
      respond to the U.S. labor market in ways that contradict traditional
      economic models of human capital theory. He posits that worker skills are
      complementary in production (i.e., firms attempt to match workers of
      similar skills) and are only imperfectly observable by firms (i.e., firms
      match workers of the same ethnicity, using county of origin as an indicator
      of skill-a feature of statistical discrimination. Thus, a worker's earnings and
      incentives for human capital accumulation depend on the average skill
      level of his ethnic group. This theory explains the following:
      a.   New immigrants cluster in locations with high concentrations of
           previous immigrants of the same nationality in order to be matched
           with more highly skilled earlier immigrants.
      b.   Immigrants from poorer sending countries receive lower entry
           earnings and lower returns to experience, even after controlling for
           measure skills because ongoing inflows of mostly unskilled new
           immigrants depress the earnings of earlier immigrants and incentives
           for skill accumulation.
      c.   Due to differences in skill investments, the earnings gaps between
           immigrants from different source countries do not vanish over time.
      d.   Larger inflows of immigrants worsen the matching prospects of
           earlier immigrants and therefore depress their earnings and skill

investments. However, native workers are only affected to the extent that immigrants are cross-matched with natives.

c. A fraction of immigrants eventually returns home, even to poor sources countries because return migration provides an additional opportunity to separate from unskilled co-workers and to signal a high skill level.

[3] Since the number of immigrants with a graduate or professional degree is relatively small compared to those who have less than a graduate degree, I assume that most immigrant adults in my final sample have been schooled outside of the United States.

[4] Male Mexicans are one notable exception. As a group, the mean education levels of male Mexican immigrants in the United States are not significantly different from the mean level of education for males in Mexico.

[5] I refrain from hypothesizing what might be causing the negative association between education and occupation for immigrant and native Whites and Other Latinos because the categorizations, by definition, are conglomerates of wide regions that include many different countries of origin.

CHAPTER 3

[1] Although attrition is often a problem in any survey design of the magnitude of NELS, my final sample does not differ dramatically in racial and ethnic proportions, or in social status of parents, from the original 1988 sample constructed by NELS administrators. I am thus quite confident that my final sample, with weights, is similar to national population measures.

[2] Accounting for clustering is necessary for "honest" estimates of standard errors, valid p-values, and confidence intervals whose true coverage is close to 95 percent. If I were to use estimators that assume independence, the standard errors would be too small – the difference can be as much as a factor of two or more. Weights are equal to (or proportional to) the inverse of the probability of being sampled. Including sampling weights in the analysis gives estimators that are approximately unbiased for whatever I attempt to estimate in the full population.

3   For more information about NELS data collection and sampling, see Hafner et al. (1990) and Haggerty et al. (1996).

4   The relative size of the coefficients for the regressions with weights and without weights are not significantly different from each other, suggesting that the weighted estimates I use in my models are not inflating the standard errors.

5   I compared responses on the 1990 U.S. Census for ethnicity and ancestry with country of origin. Most groups the same ethnic group as country of origin, except Chinese. Because the Chinese have a long history of migration, many ethnically Chinese immigrants in the United States may have been born in country outside of China or Taiwan.

6   Only three responses were dropped because of a lack of parental occupational status.

7   Ordered logistic regression is maximum likelihood estimation where an underlying score is estimated as a linear function of the independent variables and a set of "cut points." The probability of observing a particular outcome corresponds to the probability that the estimated linear function, plus random error, is within the range of cut points estimated for the outcome.

8   My analyses include divorced, separated, and married families.

9   Ruben Rumbaut's (2005) work on differences among 1st, 2nd, and 3rd generation children and the .5, 1.5, and 2.5 generation children is one notable exception. In his work, children are categorized by their country of birth, length of residence in the United States and by country of origin of their parents. For example, children who are foreign-born of foreign-born parents, but have been living in the U.S. since before entering school, are categorized as 1.5ers since they share many characteristics of their 2nd generation peers who were born in the U.S. to foreign-born parents and of their 1st generation peers who are foreign-born or foreign-born parents, but started school outside of the U.S. He argues for more research that recognizes these generational differences within immigrant populations.

[10] "Whites" have the highest mean number of people living among their co-ethnics (90.8 percent). However, because the racial categorization of white is an ethnically heterogeneous group, it is difficult to ascertain whether the whites within this category live among their own co-ethnics or with others who also claim they are "white," but are of a different ethnic group. I therefore refrain from making any general comments about who this group lives among.

[11] As an example of what the interpretation would entail, let's look at Model 1, in which there are no controls and there are only two variables in the equation and a third as the reference variable. The odds that the child's post-secondary education is greater than or equal to a given level j versus less than is estimated to be $e^{0.023}$= 1.023 times as high for respondents with one foreign-born parent as those students with both parents who are native-born. In contrast, having both parents who are foreign-born is associated with a 43-percent increase in the odds $(e^{0.355})$=1.426= 43 percent. For a student estimated as not graduating from high school, the score is less than the estimated cut point 1 (-1.615). For a student with both parents who are foreign, the probability to be categorized as having no high school degree is the probability that $0.35 + u_j <= (-1.615)$. Thus, $u_j <= -1.96$. The logistic calculations of probability is $1/(1+e-u) = 1/(1+e^{+1.96}) = 0.123$. On the other hand, for a student with only one parent who is foreign-born, the probability to be categorized as not graduating from high school is the probability that $0.023 + u_j <= (-1.615)$. Thus, $u_j <= -1.635$. The probability for a child in a combined family to be categorized as not graduating from high school is $1/(1+e^{+1.635}) = 0.163$. For a student with both parents who are native-born, the probability to be categorized as having no post-secondary education is the probability that $u_j <= (-1.615)$. $1/(1+e^{+1.615}) = 0.165$. In sum, it would be easier to state that students with both parents who are foreign-born are associated with having a higher post-secondary education (b=0.355) than students with both parents who are native-born. On the other hand, students with only one parent who is foreign-born are not more or less likely to have a higher post-secondary education (b=0.023) than are students born in a family with two native-born parents. I thus find that the likelihood of entering post-secondary schooling increases with parents both foreign-born, as compared to having two native-born parents.

[12] Imagine the three response probabilities to be the area under a normal curve partitioned into three regions by the two thresholds. These predicted

probabilities give a more detailed picture of the effect of education than simply interpreting the marginal effect on the transformed u.

CHAPTER 4

[1] One research work that investigates the interaction of immigration status and parental involvement is Pong, Hao, and Gardner (2002)'s Policy Research Institute Working Paper that looks at health behaviors for children in different immigrant generations.

[2] A third branch of research focuses on classroom-level culture. Cultural differences in the classroom may occur between the student and his or her teacher, leading to a student not being able to digest material or to learn as effectively, thus stunting that student's ability to perform well on tests or to proceed through grades. Teachers are "gatekeepers" of access to higher grade levels. In this way, culture becomes a tool to help a student maneuver through school. Due to the constraints of my data, I do not examine this conceptualization of culture.

[3] Parents from both ethnic sub-groups, however, do perceive that they talk with their children about school activities and experiences fairly often— somewhere in between "occasionally" and "regularly."

Bibliography

Ainsworth, James. 2002. "Why Does It Take a Village? The Mediation of Neighborhood Effects on Educational Achievement." *Social Forces*. vol. 81, n. 1 (117-152).

Altonji, J.G. and D. Card. 1991. "The Effects of Immigration on the Labor Market Outcomes of Less-Skilled Natives," in J.M. Abowd and R.B. Freeman (eds.) *Immigration, Trade, and the Labor Market*. Chicago: University of Chicago Press.

Azmitta, Margarita et al. 1994. *Links Between Home and School among Low-income Mexican-American and European-American Families*. Educational Practice Report No. 9. National Center for Research on Cultural Diversity and Second Language Learning: University of California, Santa Cruz.

Bailey, Thomas and Roger Waldinger. 1991. "Primary, Secondary, and Enclave Labor Markets: A Training System Approach." *American Sociological Review*, vol. 56 (386-398).

Bankston, Carl and Min Zhou. 2002a. "Social Capital as Process: The Meanings and Problems of Theoretical Metaphor." *Sociological Inquiry*, vol. 72, n. 2 (285-317).

Bankston, Carl and Min Zhou. 2002b. "Social Capital and Immigrant Children's Achievement." in *Schooling and Social Capital in Diverse Cultures*. B. Full and E. Hannum (eds). Boston: JAI/Elsevier Science.

Bankston, Carl. 2004. "Social Capital, Cultural Values, Immigration, and Academic Achievement: The Host Country Context and Contradictory Consequences." *Sociology of Education*. vol. 77 (176-179).

Barro, Robert J. and Jong-Wha Lee. 2000. *International Data on Educational Attainment: Updates and Implications.* Center for International Development Working Paper No. 42, Harvard University.

Bartel, A. 1989. "Where do the New U.S. Immigrants Live?" *Journal of Labor Economic.* vol.7 (371-391).

Bennici, F.J. and W.E. Strang. 1995. *An Analysis of Language Minority and Limited English Proficient Students from NELS:88.* Task Order D100. Washington, DC: Office of Bilingual Education and Minority Language Affairs, U.S. Department of Education.

Betts, Julian and Magnus Lofstrom. 1998. *The Educational Attainment of Immigrants: Trends and Implications.* National Bureau of Economics Research Working Paper No. W6757. October.

Bhattacharya, Gauri. 2000. "The School Adjustment of South Asian Immigrant Children in the United States." *Adolescence,* Spring, vol. 35, n. 137 (77-85).

Blau, Peter and O.D. Duncan. 1967. "The Process of Stratification." In *The American Occupational Structure.* New York, NY: Wiley (163-205).

Booth, Alan, Ann C. Crouter; and Nancy Landale (eds.). 1997. *Immigration and the Family.* Mahwah, NJ: Lawrence Erlbaum Associates.

Borjas, George. 1990. *Friends or Strangers: The Impact of Immigration on the U.S. Economy.* New York, NY: Basic Books.

Borjas, George. 1992. "Ethnic Capital and Intergenerational Mobility." *Quarterly Journal of Economics.* January, vol. 107, n. 1 (123-150).

Borjas, George. 1993. "The Intergenerational Mobility of Immigrants." *Journal of Labor Economics.* January, vol. 11, n. 1 (113-135).

Borjas, George. 1994. "The Economics of Immigration." *Journal of Economic Literature.* vol. 32 (1667-1717).

Borjas, George. 1999. *Heaven's Door: Immigration Policy and the American Economy.* Princeton, NJ: Princeton University Press.

Borjas, George. 2000. *Issues in the Economics of Immigration: A National Bureau of Economics Research Conference Report.* Chicago, IL: University of Chicago Press.

Bourdieu, Pierre and Jean-Claude Passerson. 1977. *Reproduction in Education, Society and Culture.* London, UK: Sage Publications.

Breton, Raymond. 1964. "Institutional Completeness of Ethnic Communities and the Personal Relations of Immigrants." *American Journal of Sociology,* vol. 70, n.2 (193-205).

Broeder, Peter. 1998. *Language, Ethnicity, and Education: Case Studies on Immigrant Minority Groups.* London, UK: Taylor & Francis, Inc.

Brooks-Gunn, Greg Duncan, J. Lawrence Aber (eds.) 1997. *Neighborhood Poverty.* Volumes I and II. New York: Russell Sage Foundation.

Brooks-Gunn, Jeanne, Greg Duncan, Pamela Klebanov, and Naomi Sealand. 1993. "Do Neighborhoods Influence Child and Adolescent Development?" *American Journal of Sociology.* vol. 99, n. 2 (353-395).

Buriel, Raymond and Desdemona Cardoza. 1988. "Socio-cultural Correlates of Achievement Among Three Generations of Mexican American High School Seniors." *American Educational Research Journal,* Summer, vol. 25, n. 2 (177-192).

Cafferty, Pastora San Juan and William McCready (eds.). 1985. *Hispanics in the United States.* New Brunswick, NJ: Rutgers University Press.

Camarota, Steven A. 2002. *Immigrants in the United States-2002: A Snapshot of America's Foreign-Born Population.* Washington, DC: Center For Immigration Studies, January.

Camarota, Steven. 1999. *Immigrants in the United States – 1998: A Snapshot of America's Foreign-Born Population.* Washington, DC: Center for Immigration Studies, January.

Caplan, Nathan, Marcella Choy, and John K. Whitmore. 1991. *Children of the Boat People: A Study of Educational Success.* Ann Arbor, MI: The University of Michigan Press.

Carliner, Geoffrey. 1980. "Wages, Earnings and Hours of First, Second, and Third Generation American Males." *Economic Inquiry,* January. vol. 18, n. 1 (87-102).

Caudill, W. and G. DeVos. 1956. "Achievement, Culture, and Personality: The Case of the Japanese Americans." *American Anthropologist.* vol. 58 (1102-1126).

Cheng, Li Rong Lilly. 1987. "Cross-Cultural and Linguistic Considerations in Working with Asian Populations." *ASHA,* June, vol. 29 (33-38).

Chiswick, Barry. 1977. "Sons of Immigrants: Are They at an Earnings Disadvantage?" *American Economic Review. Papers and Proceedings of the Eighty-Ninth Annual Meeting of the American Economic Association.* February, vol. 67, n. 1 (376-380).

Chiswick, Barry. 1986. "Is the New Immigration Less Skilled than the Old?" *Journal of Labor Economics,* vol. 4, n. 2 (168-192).

Coleman, James. 1987. "Families and Schools." *Educational Researcher.* vol. 16 (32-38).

Coleman, James, T. Hoffer, and S. Kilgore. 1987. *Public and Private Schools: The Impact of Communities.* New York, NY: Basic Books.

Coleman, James. 1988. "Social Capital in the Creation of Human Capital." *American Journal of Sociology*, vol. 94 (95-120).

Coleman, James. 1994. *Foundations of Social Theory*. Cambridge, MA: Belknap Press.

Collier, Virginia. 1992. "A Synthesis of Studies Examining Long-Term Language Minority Student Data on Academic Achievement." *Bilingual Research Journal*. vol. 16 (187-212).

Corcoran, Mary, Roger Gordon, Deborah Laren and Gary Solon. 1992. "The Association Between Men's Economic Status and Their Family and Community Origins." *The Journal of Human Resources*. vol. 27, n. 4 (575-601).

Crandall, J. Dale, N.C. Rhodes, and G. Spanos. 1985. "The Language of Mathematics: The English Barrier." in *Proceedings of the 1985 Delaware Symposium on Language Studies*, vol. II. Newark, DE: University of Delaware Press. (129-150).

Crowder, Kyle and Scott South. 2003. "Neighborhood Distress and School Dropout: The Variable Significance of Community Context." *Social Science Research*. vol. 32 (659-698).

Cummins, Jim. 1996. *Negotiating Identities: Education for Empowerment in a Diverse Society*. Ontario, CA: California Association for Bilingual Education.

Del Pinal, Jorge and Jesus Garcia. 1994. *Hispanic Americans Today: A Report from Census Data*. Upland, CA: DIANE Publishing Company.

DeLange, Robert. 1992. "Ethnic Background, Social Class or Social Status? Developments in School Attainment of the Children of Immigrants." *Ethnic and Racial Studies*. April, vol. 15, n. 2 (284-304).

Delgado-Gaitan, Concha and Henry Trueba. 1991. *Crossing Cultural Borders – Education for Immigrant Families in America*. Bristol, PA: Falmer Press.

DeNavas-Walt, Carmen, Bernadetter D. Proctor, and Robert J. Mills. 2004. *Income, Poverty, and Health Insurance Coverage in the United States: 2003*. U.S. Census Bureau, Current Population Reports, P60-226. U.S. Government Printing Office: Washington, D.C.

Dentler, Robert A. and Anne Hafner. 1997. *Hosting Newcomers: Structuring Educational Opportunities for Immigrant Children*. New York, NY: Teachers College Press.

Desimone, Laura. 1999. "Linking Parent Involvement with Student Achievement: do Race and Income Matter?" *The Journal of Educational Researc*. vol. 93, n. 1 (11-30).

Driscoll, Anne. 1999. "Risk of High School Dropout Among Immigrant and Native Hispanic Youth." *International Migration Review.* Winter, vol. 33, n. 4 (857-875).

Duncan, Greg. 1994. "Families and Neighborhoods as Sources of Disadvantage in the Schooling Decisions of White and Black Adolescents." *American Journal of Education.* vol. 103, n.1 (20-53).

Duncan, Greg, W. Yeung, J. Brooks-Gunn, J.R. Smith. 1998. "How Much Does Childhood Poverty Affect the Life Chances of Children?" *American Sociological Review.* vol. 63 (406-423).

Duran, Bernadine J. 1992. "Immigrants' Aspirations, High School Process, and Academic Outcomes." *American Educational Research Journal.* vol. 29, n. 1 (163).

Edmonston, Barry (ed). 1996. *Statistics of Immigration: An Assessment of Data Needs for Future Research.* Washington, DC: National Research Council.

Farkas, George, Robert Grobe, Daniel Sheehan, and Yuan Shuan. 1990. "Cultural Resources and School Success: Gender, Ethnicity, and Poverty Groups Within an Urban School District." *American Sociological Review,* February, vol. 55 (127-142).

Farkas, George. 1996. *Human Capital or Social Capital?* New York, NY: Aldine de Gruyter.

Farr, James. 2004. "Social Capital: A Conceptual History." *Political Theory.* vol. 32, n. 1 (6-33).

Featherman, D.L. and R. Hauser. 1976. "Prestige or Socioeconomic Scales in Study of Occupational Achievement." *Sociological Methods and Research,* vol. 4, n. 4 (403-422).

Fernandez, Roberto, Ronnelle Paulsen, and Marsha Hirano-Naknishi. 1989. "Dropping out Among Hispanic Youth." *Social Science Research,* vol. 18 (21-52).

Fiorina, Morris. 1999. "Extreme Voices: A Dark Side of Civic Engagement." In Skocpol and Fiorina (eds.) *Civic Engagement in American Democracy.* Washington DC: Brookings Institution Press and New York, NY: Russell Sage Foundation.

Fligstein, Neil and Roberto Fernandez. 1985. "Hispanics and Education." In P. Cafferty and W. McCready (eds.) *Hispanics in the United States.* New Brunswick, NJ: Rutgers University Press (113-146).

Flores, Judith L (ed). 1996. *Children of La Frontera: Binational Efforts to Serve Mexican Migrant and Immigrant Students.* Charleston, NC: ERIC Clearinghouse on Rural Education and Small Schools.

Foster, E.M. and S. McLanahan. 1996. "An Illustration of the Use of Instrumental Vaiables: Do Neighborhood Conditions Affect a Young Person's Changes of Finishing High School?" *Psychological Methods.* vol. 1, n.3 (249-260).

Fuligni, Andrew. 1997. "The Academic Achievement of Adolescents from Immigrant Families: The Roles of Family Background, Attitudes, and Behavior." *Child Development*, April, vol. 68 (351-368).

Ganzeboom, Harry and Donald Treiman. 1996. "Internationally Comparable Measures of Occupational Status for the 1988 International Standard Classification of Occupations." *Social Science Research,* vol. 25 (201-239).

Garrett, P., N. Ng'andu, and J. Ferron. 1994. "Poverty Experience of Young Children and the Quality of Their Home Environments." *Child Development.* vol. 65 (331-345).

Genesee, Fred (ed.). 1999. *Program Alternatives for Linguistically Diverse Students.* Santa Cruz, CA: Center For Research on Education, Diversity and Excellence.

Ghasarian, Christian. 1995. "Education and Its Consequences: Value Conflicts in an Immigrant Community." *Social Education.* February, vol. 59 (78-81).

Ghuman, Paul A. Singh. 1997. "Assimilation or Integration? A Study of Asian Adolescents." *Educational Research.* Spring, vol. 39, n. 1 (23-36).

Gibson, Margaret and John Ogbu (eds.). 1991. *Minority Status and Schooling: A Comparative Study of Immigrant and Involuntary Minorities.* New York, NY: Garland.

Gibson, Margaret. 1988. *Accommodation without Assimilation: Punjabi Sikh Immigrants in an American High School and Community.* Ithaca, NY: Cornell University Press.

Glick, Jennifer and Michael White. 2003. "The Academic Trajectories of Immigrant Youths: Analysis Within and Across Cohorts." *Demography.* vol. 40, n. 4 (759-783).

Gordon, Milton. 1964. *Assimilation in American Life: The Role of Race, Religion, and National Origin.* New York, NY: Oxford University Press.

Gottfredson, Denise. 1981. "Black-White Differences in the Educational Attainment Process: What Have We Learned?" *American Sociological Review,* vol. 64, n. 5 (542-557).

Grant, Linda and Xue Lan Rong. 1992. "Gender, Immigrant Generation, Ethnicity and the Schooling Progress of Youth." *Journal of Research and Development in Education*, Fall, vol. 33, n. 1 (15-26).

Grenier, Gilles. 1984. "The Effects of Language Characteristics on the Wages of Hispanic-American Males. *The Journal of Human Resources.* vol. 19, n. 1 (35-52).

Hafner, Anne, Steven Ingels, Barbara Schneider, and David Stevenson. 1990. *National Education Longitudinal Study of 1988: A Profile of The American Eighth Grader: NELS:88 Student Descriptive Summary.* National Center for Education Statistics No. 90-458. Washington, DC: U.S. Department of Education.

Hagan, John, Ross MacMillan, and Blair Wheaton. 1996. "New Kid in Town: Social Capital and the Life Course Effects of Migration on Children." *American Sociological Review,* vol. 61, n. 3 (368-385).

Haggerty, Catherine, Bernard Dugoni, Laura Reed, Ann Cederlund, and John Taylor. 1996. *National Education Longitudinal Study: 1988-1994 Methodology Report.* National Center for Education Statistics. No. 96-174. Washington, DC: U.S. Department of Education, March.

Haller, Archibald and Alejandro Portes. 1973. "Status Attainment Processes." *Sociology of Education,* vol. 46 (51-91).

Hao, Lingxin and Melissa Bonstead-Bruns. 1998. "Parent-child Differences in Educational Expectations and the Academic Achievement of Immigrant and Native Students." *Sociology of Education,* July, vol. 71, n. 3 (175-198).

Hayes, Katherine. 1992. "Attitudes Toward Education: Voluntary and Involuntary Immigrants From the Same Family." *Anthropology and Education Quarterly,* September, vol. 23 (250-267).

Henderson, R.W. 1980. "Social and Emotional Needs of Culturally Diverse Children." *Exceptional Children,* vol. 46 (598-604).

Hendricks, Lutz. 2001. "The Economic Performance of Immigrants: A Theory of Assortative Matching." *International Economic Review.* v. 42, n. 2 (May): 417-449.

Hickey, M. Gail. 1998. "'Back Home, Nobody'd Do That': Immigrant Students and Cultural Models of Schooling with Emphasis on Asian and Hispanic Children." *Social Education,* November/December, vol. 62, n. 7 (442-447).

Hirschman, Charles. 2001. "The Educational Enrollment of Immigrant Youth: A Test of the Segmented Assimilation Hypothesis." *Demography.* August, vol. 38, n. 3 (317-336).

Hodgkinson, H.L. 1992. *A Demographic Look at Tomorrow.* Washington, DC: Institute for Educational Leadership, Center for Demographic Policy.

Holman, Linda Jean. 1997. "Meeting the Needs of Hispanic Immigrants." *Educational Leadershi,* April, vol. 54 (37-38).

Hones, Donald and Shou Cha. 1999. *Educating New Americans: Immigrant Lives and Learning.* Mahwah, NJ: Lawrence Erlbaum Associates, Inc.

Hurtado, A. and E. Garcia. 1994. *The Educational Achievement of Latinos: Barriers and Successes.* Santa Cruz, CA: University of California.

Ingels, Steven J. 1996. *Sample Exclusion in NELS:88. Characteristics of Base Year Ineligible Students; Changes in Eligibility Status After Four Years.* National Center for Education Statistics. Technical Report No. 96-723. Washington, DC: U.S. Department of Education, May.

Inger, Morton. 1992. "Increasing the School Involvement of Hispanic Parents." *ERIC Digest: Clearinghouse on Urban Education.* August, no. 80.

Israel, Glenn, Lionel Beaulieu, and Glen Hartless. 2001. "The Influence of Family and Community Social Capital on Educational Achievement." *Rural Sociology.* vol. 66, n. 1 (43-68).

Jones, Frank. 1987. "Age at Immigration and Education – Further Explorations." *International Migration Review,* Spring, vol. 21, n. 1 (70-85).

Kao, Grace. 1999. "Psychological Well-being and Educational Achievement Among Immigrant Youth." In J. Hernandez (ed) *Children of Immigrants: Health, Adjustments and Public Assistance.* Washington, DC: National Academy Press.

Kao, Grace. 2004. "Social Capital and Its Relevance to Minority and Immigrant Populations." *Sociology of Education.* April, vol. 77 (172-175).

Kao, Grace and Jennifer Thompson. 2003. "Racial and Ethnic Stratification in Educational Achievement and Attainment." *Annual Review of Sociology.* vol. 29 (417-442).

Kao, Grace and Marta Tienda. 1995. "Optimism and Achievement: The Educational Performance of Immigrant Youth." *Social Science Quarterly.* March, vol. 76, n. 1 (1-20).

Kaufman, Phillip, Lisa Chavez, and Douglas Lauen. 1998. *Generational Status and Educational Outcomes Among Asian and Hispanic 1988 Eighth Graders.* National Center for Education Statistics Statistical Analysis Report No. 1999-020. Washington, DC: U.S. Department of Education, September.

Kessler, Carolyn. 1987. "Linking Mathematics and Second Language Learning." Paper presented to the Annual Meeting of the Teachers of English to Speakers of Other Languages. April. Miami Beach, FL.

Kim, Rebecca. 2002. "Ethnic Differences in Academic Achievement Between Vietnamese and Cambodian Children: Cultural and Structural Explanations." *The Sociological Quarterly.* vol. 43, n.2 (213-235).

Kurtz Costes, Beth and Elizabeth Pungello. 2000. "Acculturation and Immigrant Children: Implications for Educators." *Social Education,* March, vol. 64, n. 2 (121-125).

LaLonde, R and R. Topel. 1991. "Labor Market Adjustments to Increased Immigration," in J.M. Abowd and R.B. Freeman (eds.) *Immigration, Trade, and the Labor Market.* Chicago: University of Chicago Press.

Lamont, Michele and Annette Lareau. 1988. "Cultural Capital: Allusions, Gaps, and Glissandos in Recent Theoretical Developments." *Sociological Theory,* vol. 16, n. 2 (153-168).

Lapham, Susan. 1993. *We, The American Foreign Born.* Ethnic and Hispanic Branch, Population Division. Washington, DC: Bureau of the Census.

Lareau, Annette. 1989. *Home Advantage: Social Class and Parental Intervention in Elementary Education.* Philadelphia, PA: Falmer Press.

Larsen, Luke. J. 2004. *The Foreign-Born Population in the United States: 2003.* Current Population Reports, P20-551. U.S. Census Bureau, Washington, D.C.

Lee, Everett S. and Xue-lan Rong. 1988. "The Educational and Economic Achievement of Asian-Americans." *The Elementary School Journal,* vol. 88, n. 5 (545-560).

Light, Ivan. 1984. "Immigrant and Ethnic Enterprise in North America." *Ethnic and Racial Studies,* vol. 7 (195-216).

Lollock, Lisa. 2001. "The Foreign-Born Population in the United States: March 2000." *Current Population Reports,* P20-534. Washington, DC: U.S. Census Bureau.

Lucas, Tamara. 1996. *Promoting Secondary School Transitions for Immigrant Adolescents.* ERIC Digest: Clearinghouse on Languages and Linguistics. December. http://www.cal.org.ericcll/digest/Lucas001.htm (also in High School Magazine, Jan/ Feb, 1999, vol. 6, no. 4 (40-41)).

Mace-Matluck, Betty, Rosalind Alexander-Kasparik, and Robin M. Queen. 1998. "Qualities of Effective Programs for Immigrant Adolescents with Limited Schooling." ERIC Digest: Clearinghouse on Languages and Linguistics. November. From *Through the Golden Door: Educational Approaches for Immigrant Adolescents with Limited Schooling.* Delta Systems, Co., Inc. http://www.cal.org.ericcll/digest/goldendoor.html.

Malloy, Carol E and William Malloy. 1998. "Issues of Culture in Mathematics Teaching and Learning". *The Urban Review*, September, vol. 30, n. 3 (245-257).

Mare, R. and C. Winship. 1988. "Ethnic and Racial Patterns of Educational Attainment and School Enrollment." In Gary Sandefur and Marta Tienda (eds.) *Divided Opportunities: Minorities, Poverty, and Social Policy.* New York, NY: Garland. (173-203).

Marjoribanks, Kevin. 2003. "A Research Note: Immigrant Adolescents' Individual and Environmental Influences on Young Adults' Educational Attainment." *Journal of Comparative Family Studies.* vol. 35, n.3 (485-499).

Matute-Bianchi, Maria Eugenia. 1986. "Ethnic Identities and Patterns of School Success and Failure among Mexican-Descent and Japanese-American Students in a California High School: An Ethnographic Analysis." *American Journal of Education*, November (233-255).

Mau, Wei Cheng. 1997. "Parental Influences on the High School Students' Academic Achievement: A Comparison of Asian Immigrants, Asian Americans, and White Americans." *Psychology in the Schools.* July, vol. 34 (267-277).

McCargo, Cathleen. 1999. "Addressing the Needs of English-Language Learners in Science and Math Classrooms." *The ERIC Review: K-8 Science and Mathematics Education.* Fall, vol. 6, n. 2 (52-54).

McDonnell, Lorraine and Paul T. Hill. 1993. *Newcomers in American Schools: Meeting the Educational Needs of Immigrant Youth.* Santa Monica, CA: RAND.

McNeal, Ralph. 1999. "Parental Involvement as Social Capital: Differential Effectiveness on Science Achievement, Truancy, and Dropping Out." *Social Forces.* vol. 78, n. 1 (117-144).

Mehan, Hugh. 1997. *Contextual Factors Surrounding Hispanic Dropouts.* January. Prepared for the Hispanic Dropout Project. http://www.ncbe.edu/miscpubs/hdp/1/index.htm.

Morgan, Stephen and Aage Sørensen. 1999. "Parental Networks, Social Closure, and Mathematics Learning: A Test of Coleman's Social Capital Explanation of School Effects." *American Sociological Review.* vol. 65, n.5 (661-682).

Morris, Nancy. 1995. *Puerto Rico: Culture, Politics, and Identity.* Westport, CT: Praeger Publications.

Morse, Susan. 1990. "The Non-Schooled Immigrant Child." *Thrust*, January, vol. 19 (36-38).

Muller, Chandra. 1993. "Parent Involvement and Academic Achievement: An Analysis of Family Resources Available to the Child", in B. Schneider and J. Coleman (eds.) *Parents, Their Children, and Schools*. Boulder, CO: Westview. (77-114).

Muller, Chandra. 1995. "Maternal Employment, Parent Involvement, and Mathematics Achievement among Adolescents." *Journal of Marriage and the Family*. vol 571, n. 1 (85-100).

Noguera, Pedro. 2004. "Social Capital and the Education of Immigrant Students: Categories and Generalizations." *Sociology of Education*. April, vol. 77 (180-183).

Ogbu, John and Herbert Simons. 1998. "Voluntary and Involuntary Minorities: A Cultural-Ecological Theory of School Performance with Some Implications for Education." *Anthropology and Education Quarterly*, June, vol. 29, n. 2 (155-188).

Ogbu, John. 1991. "Immigrant and Involuntary Minorities in Comparative Perspective." in Margaret Gibson and John Ogbu (eds.) *Minority Status and Schooling: A Comparative Study of Immigrant and Involuntary Minorities*. New York, NY: Garland Publishers (3-33).

Park, Robert. 1914. "Racial Assimilation in Secondary Groups with Particular Reference to the Negro." *American Journal of Sociology*, vol. 19, n. 5 (606-623).

Perkins, Linda Marie. 2000. "The New Immigrants and Education: Challenges and Issues." *Educational Horizons*. Winter, vol. 78, n. 2 (67-71).

Perlmann, Joel and Roger Waldinger. 1996. "The Second Generation and the Children of the Native-born: Comparisons and Refinements." Working Paper no. 174.

Pettit, M. and S. McLanahan. 2003. "Residential Mobility and Children's Social Capital: Evidence from an Experiment." *Social Science Quarterly*. vol. 84, n. 3 (632-649).

Pong, Suet-Ling, Lingxin Hao, and Erica Gardner. 2002. *Parental Involvement in Children's Educational Achievement: Immigration Generational Differences*. Population Research Institute Working Paper 02-05. August.

Portes, Alejandro (ed.). 1995. *The Economics of Sociology: Essays on Networks, Ethnicity, and Entrepreneurship*. New York, NY: Russell Sage Foundation.

Portes, Alejandro and Dag MacLeod. 1996. "Educational Progress of Children of Immigrants: the Roles of Class, Ethnicity, and School Context." *Sociology of Education*, October, vol. 69 (255-275).

Portes, Alejandro and József Böröcz. 1991. "Contemporary Immigration: Theoretical Perspectives on Its Determinants and Modes of Incorporation." *International Migration Review*, vol. 23, n. 3 (606-630).

Portes, Alejandro and Mihn Zhou. 1993. "The New Second Generation: Segmented Assimilation and its Variants." *Annals of the American Academy of Political and Social Sciences*, vol. 530 (75-96).

Portes, Alejandro and R. Stepick. 1993. *City on the Edge: The Transformation of Miami*. Berkeley, CA: University of California Press.

Portes, Alejandro and Ruben Rumbaut. 1996. *Immigrant America: A Portrait*. Berkeley, CA: University of California Press.

Portes, Alejandro. 1996. "The Educational Progress of Children of Immigrants: The Roles of Class, Ethnicity, and School Context." *Sociology of Education*. October, vol. 69, n. 4 (255-276).

Portes, Alejandro. 1998. "Social Capital: Its Origins and Applications in Modern Sociology." *Annual Review of Sociology*, vol. 24 (1-24).

Portes, Pedro R. 1999. "Social and Psychological Factors in the Academic Achievement of Children of Immigrants: A Cultural History Puzzle." *American Educational Research Journal*. Fall, vol. 36, n. 3 (489-507).

Putnam, Robert. 2000. *Bowling Alone: The Collapse and Revival of American Community*. New York, NY: Simon and Schuster.

Ray, Douglas and Deo Poonwassie (eds.) 1992. *Education and Cultural Differences: New Perspective*. New York, NY: Garland Publishing.

Ream, Robert. 2003. "Counterfeit Social Capital and Mexican-American Underachievement." *Educational Evaluation and Policy Analysis*. vol. 25, n. 3 (237-262).

Rivera-Batiz, Francisco and Carlos Santiago. 1998. *Island Paradox: Puerto Rico in the 1990s*. New York, NY: Russell Sage Foundation.

Rong, Xue Lan and Judith Preissle. 1998. *Educating Immigrant Students: What We Need to Know to Meet the Challenges*. Thousand Oaks, CA: Corwin Press.

Rong, Xue Lan and Linda Grant. 1992. "Ethnicity, Generation, and School Attainment of Asians, Hispanics, and Non-Hispanic Whites." *The Sociological Quarterly*. vol. 33, n. 4 (625-636).

Rong, Xue Lan and M. Gail Hickey. 1998. "Focusing on the New Immigration." *Social Education*, November/December, vol. 62, n. 7 (390-392).

Roscigno, Vincent. 1999. "The Black-White Achievement Gap, Family-School Links, and the Importance of Place." *Sociological Inquiry*. vol. 69 (159-86).

Rumbaut, Ruben and Kenji Ima. 1988. *The Adaptation of Southeast Asian Refugee Youth: A Comparative Study.* Washington, DC: Office of Refugee Resettlement.

Rumbaut, Ruben G. 2004. "Ages, Life Stages, and Generational Cohorts: Decomposing the Immigrant First and Second Generations in the United States." *International Migration Review.* vol. 38, n. 3 (1160-1206).

Rumbaut, Ruben. 1994. "The Crucible Within: Ethnic Identity, Self-Esteem and Segmented Assimilation Among Children of Immigrants." *International Migration Review.* vol. 28, n. 4 (748-794).

Rumbaut, Ruben. 1997. "Assimilation and Its Discontents: Between Rhetoric and Reality. *International Migration Review.* vol. 31, n. 4 (923-960).

Rumberger, Russell and Katherine Larson. 1998. "Toward Explaining Differences in Educational Achievement among Mexican American Language-Minority Students. *Sociology of Education.* January, vol. 71 (69-93).

Rutledge, Paul. 1992. *The Vietnamese Experience in America.* Bloomington: Indiana University Press.

Sampson, Robert, Jeffrey Morenoff, Thomas Gannon-Rowley. 2002. "Assessing "Neighborhood Effects": Social Processes and New Directions in Research." *Annual Review of Sociology.* vol. 28 (443-78).

Sampson, Robert. 1991. "Linking the Micro- and Macrolevel Dimensions of Community Social Organization. *Social Forces.* vol. 70, n.1 (43-64).

Schmid, Carol. 2001. "Educational Achievement, Language-Minority Students, and the New Second Generation." *Sociology of Education.* vol. 74, extra issue (71-87).

Schmidley, Dianne A. 2001. *Profile of the Foreign-Born Population in the United States: 2000.* Current Population Reports, P23-206. U.S. Census Bureau, Washington, D.C.

Schmidley, Dianne A. and Gregory Robins. 2003. *Measuring the Foreign-Born Population in the United States with the Current Population Survey: 1994-2002.* Population Division Working Paper No. 73. U.S. Census Bureau, Washington, D.C.

Schneider, Barbara and Yongsook Lee. 1990. "A Model for Academic Success: The School and Home Environment of East Asian Students." *Anthropology and Education Quarterly.* December, vol. 21 (358-377).

Secada, Walter, et al. 1998. *No More Excuses: The Final Report of the Hispanic Dropout Project.* Washington, DC: U.S. Department of Education, February.

Sewell, William, Robert Hauser, and David Featherman. 1976. *Schooling and Achievement in American Society.* New York, NY: Academic Press.

Sewell, William, Robert Hauser, and Wendy Wolf. 1980. "Sex, Schooling, and Occupational Status." *American Journal of Sociology,* vol. 86, n. 3 (551-583).

Singh, Kusum, P.G. Bickley, P. Trivette, T.Z. Keith, P.B. Keith, and E. Anderson. 1995. "The Effects of Four Components of Parental Involvement on Eighth-Grade Student Achievement: Structural Analysis of NELS-88 Data." *School Psychology Review.* vol. 23, n. 1 (299-317).

Skocpol, Theda and Morris Fiorina (eds.) *Civic Engagement in American Democracy.* Washington, DC: Brookings Institution Press and New York, NY: Russell Sage Foundation.

Smith, Frances M. and Cheryl Hausafus. 1998. "Relationship of Family Support and Ethnic Minority Students' Achievement in Science and Mathematics." *Science Education,* January, vol. 82 (111-125).

Spenner, Kenneth and David Featherman. 1978. "Achievement Ambitions." *Annual Review of Sociology,* vol. 4 (373-420).

Stanic, George. 1989. "Social Inequality, Cultural Discontinuity, and Equity in School Mathematics." *Peabody Journal of Education,* vol. 66, no. 2 (57-71).

Staton-Salazar, Ricardo and Sanford Dornbusch. 1995. "Social Capital and the Reproduction of Inequality: Information Networks Among Mexican-Origin High School Students." *Sociology of Education.* April, vol. 68, no. 2 (116-136).

Steinberg, Laurence, Sanford Dornbusch, and B. Bradford Brown. 1992. "Ethnic Differences in Adolescent Achievement: An Ecological Perspective." *American Psychologist.* June, vol. 4, no. 6 (723-729).

Stevenson, D. and D. Baker. 1987. "The Family-School Relation and the Child's School Performance." *Child Development.* vol. 58 (1348-1357).

Stewart, David. 1993. *Immigration and Education: The Crises and the Opportunities.* Lanham, PA: Lexington Books.

Suárez-Orozco, Carola and Marcelo Suárez-Orozco. 2001. *Children of Immigrants.* Cambridge, MA: Harvard University Press.

Suárez-Orozco, Marcelo and Carola Suárez-Orozco. 1995. *Transformations: Immigration, Family Life, and Achievement Motivation among Latino Adolescents.* Stanford, CA: Stanford University Press.

Suárez-Orozco, Marcelo. 1987. " 'Becoming Somebody' – Central American Immigrants in U.S. Inner-city Schools." *Anthropology and Education Quarterly,* vol. 18, n. 4 (287-299, 368-382).

Suárez-Orozco, Marcelo. 1989. *Central American Refugees and U.S. High Schools: A Psychosocial Study of Motivation and Achievement.* Palo Alto, CA: Stanford University Press.

Sui-Chui, Ho and J. D. Willms. 1996. "Effects of Parent Involvement on Eighth-Grade Achievement." *Sociology of Education.* vol. 69, n. 2 (126-141).

Thomas, Tania. 1992. "Psychoeducational Adjustment of English-speaking Caribbean and Central American Immigrant Children in the United States." *The School Psychology Review,* vol. 21, n. 4 (566-576).

Usdanskey, Margaret L. and Thomas J. Espenshade. 2000. *The H-1B Visa Debate in Historical Perspective: The Evolution of U.S. Policy Toward Foreign Born.* Working Paper no. 11. San Diego, CA: The Center for Comparative Immigration Studies.

Valenzuela, Angela and Sanford Dornbusch. 1994."Familism and Social Capital in the Academic Achievements of Mexican Origin and Anglo Adolescents." *Social Science Quarterly,* vol. 75, n. 1 (18-36).

Vasquez, J. 1990. "Teaching to the Distinctive Traits of Minority Students." *The Clearing House,* vol. 63, n. 7 (299-304).

Vaznaugh, Adriana. 1995. *Dropout Intervention and Language Minority Youth.* ERIC Digest: Clearinghouse on Languages and Linguistics, March. http://www.cal.org.ericcll/digest/Vaznau01.htm

Vernez, Georges. 1996. *How Immigrants Fare in U.S. Education.* Santa Monica, CA: RAND.

Villanueva, I. 1996. *The Voices of Chicano Families: Cultural Awareness versus Acculturation and Assimilation.* Paper presented at annual meeting of the American Educational Research Association, New York, NY.

Wang, Jia and Pete Goldschmidt. 1999. "Opportunity to Learn, Language Proficiency, and Immigrant Status Effects on Mathematics Achievement." *The Journal of Education Research.* November/December, vol. 93, n. 2 (101-111).

Warren, J.R. 1996. "Educational Inequality Among White and Mexican-origin Adolescents in the American Southwest: 1990." *Sociology of Education.* April, vol. 69 (142-158).

Waters, Mary and Karl Eschbach. 1995. "Immigration and Ethnic and Racial Inequality in the United States." *Annual Review of Sociology.* vol. 21 (419-446).

Waters, Mary. 1997. "Immigrant Families at Risk: Factors that Undermine Chances for Success" in Alan Booth, Ann C. Crouter, and Nancy Landale (eds.) *Immigration and the Family.* Mahwah, NJ: Lawrence Erlbaum Associates.

Waters, Mary. 2001. *Black Identities: West Indian Immigrant Dreams and American Realities.* New York, NY: Russell Sage Foundation.

White, Michael and Gayle Kaufman. 1997. "Language Usage, Social Capital, and School Completion among Immigrants and Native-Born Ethnic Groups." *Social Science Quarterly.* vol. 78, n. 2 (385-416).

White, Michael. 1997. "Excerpt from Executive Summary and Chapter Four from Language Proficiency, Schooling and the Achievement of Immigrants." *Report to the U.S. Department of Labor.* April.

Wirt, John, et al. 2000. *The Condition of Education 2000.* National Center for Education Statistics. Washington, DC: Department of Education. NCES 2000-062.

Wojtkiewicz, Roger and Katherine Donato. 1995. "Hispanic Educational Attainment: The Effects of Family Background and Nativity." *Social Forces.* December, vol. 74, n. 2 (559-575).

Wong, Sau Ling Cynthia. 1987. "The Language Situation of Asian Immigrant Students in the U.S.: A Socio- and Psycholinguistic Perspective." *NABE Journal.* Spring, vol. 11 (203-234).

Yao, Esther Lee. 1987. "Asian-Immigrant Students: Unique Problems that Hamper Learning." *NASSP Bulletin.* December, vol. 71 (82-88).

Zhou, Min and Carl Bankston. 1994 "Social Capital and the Adaptation of the Second Generation: The Case of Vietnamese Youth in New Orleans." *International Migration Review.* vol. 28 (821-845).

Zhou, Min. 1992. *New York's Chinatown: The Socio-economic Potential of an Urban Enclave.* Philadelphia, PA: Temple University Press.

Zhou, Min. 1997. "Growing Up American: The Challenge Confronting Immigrant Children and Children of Immigrants." *Annual Review of Sociology.* vol. 23 (63-95).

Zhou, Min. 2001. "Immigrant Neighborhoods in Los Angeles: Structural Constraints and the Ethnic Resource for the Adaptation of Immigrant Children." Unpublished manuscript.

Zsembik, Barbara and Daniel Llanes. 1996. "Generational Differences in Educational Attainment among Mexican Americans." *Social Science Quarterly.* vol. 77, n. 2 (363-375).

Index